"Digital Balance: Mastering Wellness in a Screen-Centric World"

Introduction: Navigating the Digital Age

Welcome, dear reader, to a journey that's as exciting as it is essential in our modern world. Whether you're reading this on a smartphone, tablet, or good old-fashioned paper, you're already part of the digital age – an era that's revolutionized how we live, work, and connect. But like any revolution, it comes with its own set of challenges and opportunities.

I'm thrilled you've picked up this book. Perhaps you're feeling overwhelmed by the constant ping of notifications, or you're concerned about how much time your kids are spending on screens. Maybe you're experiencing mysterious aches and pains from long hours at the computer, or you're simply curious about how to make technology work better for you. Whatever brought you here, you're in the right place.

As someone who's spent years researching, writing about, and personally grappling with digital wellness, I can tell you this: finding balance in our digital lives isn't just possible – it's crucial for our health, happiness, and productivity in the 21st century.

Now, let's address the elephant in the room – or should I say, the smartphone in our hands. Technology isn't the enemy. The devices and platforms we use every day have opened up incredible possibilities. They've connected us across vast distances, democratized information, and created new forms of art and expression. The goal isn't to abandon these tools, but to use them mindfully and purposefully.

In this book, we'll explore every facet of digital wellness. We'll dive into the physical effects of screen time – yes, "tech neck" is a real thing! – and learn practical strategies to protect our bodies. We'll tackle the mental health challenges of the digital age, from social media anxiety to information overload, and discover how to cultivate a healthier online environment.

But we won't stop there. We'll also explore how technology affects our relationships, our work-life balance, and even our sleep patterns. We'll look at the latest research on blue light and learn how to adjust our devices for better eye health. And because digital wellness isn't one-size-fits-all, we'll examine how these issues affect different generations and cultures.

One of the most exciting parts of our journey will be exploring how AI and emerging technologies are shaping the future of digital wellness. From productivity tools to mental health chatbots, we'll see how technology itself can be part of the solution.

Throughout this book, you'll find practical tips, real-life examples, and interactive exercises to help you create your own digital wellness plan. Whether you're a digital native or a tech novice, there's something here for you.

Remember, the goal isn't perfection. It's progress. Small, consistent changes can make a big difference in how we interact with our digital world. By the time you finish this book, you'll have the knowledge and tools to navigate the digital age with confidence, intention, and yes, even joy.

So, are you ready to embark on this adventure towards digital balance? Let's power up and dive in – mindfully, of course!

Chapter 1: Understanding Digital Wellness:

Welcome to the first step in our journey towards digital balance. In this chapter, we'll lay the foundation for understanding what digital wellness really means and why it's so crucial in today's hyper-connected world.

Defining Digital Wellness

Digital wellness isn't about completely unplugging or shunning technology. Rather, it's about cultivating a healthy, intentional relationship with our digital tools. It encompasses how we interact with technology in ways that support our physical, mental, and emotional well-being.

Think of digital wellness as a state where you're in control of your technology use, rather than feeling controlled by it. It's about using digital tools to enhance your life, not detract from it.

The Digital Landscape Today

Let's take a moment to appreciate just how pervasive digital technology has become in our lives. From smartphones that wake us up in the morning to smart home devices that turn off our lights at night, we're surrounded by screens and connected devices.

According to recent statistics, the average person spends over 6 hours a day interacting with digital media. That's a quarter of our day! While this connectivity brings incredible benefits, it also presents new challenges to our well-being.

The Impact on Our Lives

The digital revolution has transformed nearly every aspect of our existence:

- Work: Remote work and digital collaboration tools have redefined the workplace.
- Education: Online learning platforms have opened up new educational opportunities.
- Social Interactions: Social media has changed how we connect and communicate.
- Entertainment: Streaming services and mobile games offer endless entertainment options.

- Health: Wearable devices and health apps help us monitor our physical well-being.

While these changes bring many positives, they also come with potential downsides. Information overload, digital addiction, cyberbullying, and privacy concerns are just a few of the challenges we face in the digital age.

Why Digital Wellness Matters

Achieving digital wellness is about more than just reducing screen time. It's about creating a balanced, healthy relationship with technology that enhances our overall quality of life. Here's why it matters:

1. Mental Health: Excessive or unhealthy tech use has been linked to increased stress, anxiety, and depression.
2. Physical Health: Too much screen time can lead to issues like eye strain, poor posture, and disrupted sleep patterns.
3. Relationships: Overuse of digital devices can interfere with face-to-face interactions and intimacy.
4. Productivity: Constant digital distractions can significantly impact our ability to focus and get things done.
5. Personal Growth: Spending too much time in the digital world can limit our real-world experiences and personal development.

The Digital Wellness Spectrum

It's important to understand that digital wellness isn't a binary state – you're not simply "well" or "unwell." Instead, think of it as a spectrum. On one end, you have problematic use that negatively impacts your life. On the other, you have mindful, intentional use that enhances your well-being.

Throughout this book, we'll explore strategies to move you towards the positive end of this spectrum, helping you harness the benefits of technology while minimizing its potential drawbacks.

Looking Ahead

As we delve deeper into the world of digital wellness, remember that the goal isn't perfection. It's about progress and finding what works best for you. In the coming chapters, we'll explore specific aspects of digital wellness, from physical health impacts to mental well-being, and provide practical strategies for creating a healthier digital life.

Your journey to digital wellness starts now. Are you ready to take control of your digital life and find a balance that works for you? Let's continue this exciting journey together!

Digital wellness:

Refers to the state of achieving and maintaining a healthy, balanced relationship with digital technologies that supports our overall well-being - physically, mentally, and emotionally. It involves using technology intentionally and mindfully in ways that enhance our lives rather than detract from them.

Key aspects of digital wellness include:

1. Intentional use: Using digital tools purposefully to support our goals and values, rather than letting them control us.

2. Balance: Finding an equilibrium between online and offline activities, ensuring technology use doesn't overshadow real-world experiences and relationships.

3. Physical health: Managing the physical impacts of technology use, such as eye strain, posture issues, and sleep disruption.

4. Mental health: Addressing the psychological effects of digital engagement, including stress, anxiety, and information overload.

5. Digital literacy: Understanding how to navigate the digital world safely and effectively, including evaluating online information critically.

6. Boundaries: Setting limits on technology use and creating tech-free times and spaces.

7. Positive engagement: Using digital platforms to foster meaningful connections and personal growth.

8. Safety and privacy: Protecting personal information and maintaining a positive digital footprint.

9. Productivity: Leveraging technology to enhance work efficiency while minimizing distractions.

10. Adaptability: Staying flexible in our approach to technology as it continues to evolve.

Digital wellness isn't about completely avoiding technology, but rather about cultivating a relationship with digital tools that enhances our quality of life. It's about being in control of our technology use, rather than feeling controlled by it.

As we navigate the increasingly digital landscape of modern life, understanding and practicing digital wellness becomes crucial for maintaining our overall health and happiness. It's a dynamic, ongoing process of evaluating and adjusting our digital habits to ensure they align with our personal values and contribute positively to our well-being.

The importance of balance in the digital era:

This cannot be overstated. As we navigate an increasingly connected world, finding equilibrium between our digital and physical lives has become crucial for our overall well-being. Here's why striking this balance is so important:

Preserving Mental Health

In the digital age, constant connectivity can lead to information overload and mental fatigue. Balancing our digital consumption helps to:

- Reduce stress and anxiety associated with constant notifications and social media pressures
- Prevent digital addiction and compulsive behaviors
- Allow time for mental rest and recovery

Enhancing Physical Well-being

Excessive screen time can have detrimental effects on our physical health. Achieving balance helps to:

- Reduce the risk of sedentary lifestyle-related health issues

- Prevent eye strain and other vision problems associated with prolonged screen use
- Promote better sleep patterns by limiting blue light exposure before bedtime

Nurturing Real-world Relationships

While digital platforms offer unprecedented connectivity, they can also lead to social isolation. Balance is key to:

- Fostering meaningful face-to-face interactions
- Developing and maintaining strong interpersonal skills
- Creating deeper, more authentic connections with others

Boosting Productivity and Creativity

Constant digital engagement can hinder our ability to focus and think creatively. Finding balance allows us to:

- Improve concentration and deep work capabilities
- Stimulate creativity through diverse, offline experiences
- Enhance problem-solving skills by disconnecting from digital distractions

Cultivating Mindfulness and Self-awareness

The digital world can often pull us away from the present moment. Striking a balance helps us:

- Develop greater self-awareness and emotional intelligence
- Practice mindfulness and appreciate our surroundings
- Engage more fully in our daily experiences

Protecting Privacy and Security

Overexposure in the digital realm can compromise our personal information. Balance is crucial for:

- Maintaining control over our digital footprint
- Reducing the risk of cybersecurity threats
- Preserving a sense of personal privacy in an increasingly public world

Promoting Digital Literacy and Critical Thinking

By consciously balancing our digital engagement, we can:

- Develop better digital literacy skills
- Enhance our ability to critically evaluate online information
- Make more informed decisions about our technology use

In conclusion, the importance of balance in the digital era lies in its ability to protect our mental and physical health, nurture our relationships, boost our productivity, and enhance our overall quality of life. As we continue to embrace the benefits of technology, maintaining this balance becomes not just important, but essential for thriving in the modern world.

Current trends and statistics:

Based on the search results and our previous discussion, here are some current trends and statistics in digital wellness:

1. Market Growth:
   The global digital wellness market is expected to reach over USD 1354.68 billion by 20302. This significant growth is driven by increasing smartphone penetration and the growing number of health and fitness-related applications.

2. Surge in Online Wellness Services:
   There has been a notable increase in the use of online wellness services, including telemedicine, mental health apps, and digital fitness platforms.

3. Focus on Mental Health:
   Mental health has become a primary focus in digital wellness. There's a rise in mobile mental health support and apps dedicated to mindfulness, meditation, and digital therapy14.

4. Personalized Health Guidance:
   Wearable devices and smart technology are enabling more personalized health recommendations based on individual data.

5. Medical Internet of Things (IoT):
   The adoption of cloud services, integrated apps, wearable technology, AI, and machine learning is changing healthcare delivery, allowing for remote patient monitoring and reducing the need for in-person appointments.

6. Workplace Digital Wellness:
   Employers are increasingly prioritizing digital wellness to increase health and engagement among employees. This includes providing access to wellness apps and implementing screen time awareness tools.

7. Digital Detoxing:
   There's a growing trend of people seeking ways to "digitally detox" and find balance in their technology use.

8. Sleep Technology:
   There's a major emphasis on sleep technologies and optimizing circadian rhythms as part of overall digital wellness.

9. Preventive Digital Wellness:
   There's a shift towards using digital tools for preventive health measures rather than just treatment.

10. Addressing Disparities:
   There's an increasing focus on addressing racial and economic differences in access to and use of digital health services, particularly in telehealth.

These trends indicate a growing awareness of the importance of digital wellness and an increasing integration of digital tools in various aspects of health and wellness. The statistics show a rapidly expanding market, suggesting that digital wellness will continue to be a significant focus in the coming years.

Digital wellness across generations and cultures:

Digital wellness across generations and cultures is a complex and nuanced topic, as different age groups and cultural backgrounds interact with and perceive technology in varied ways. Here's an overview of how digital wellness manifests across generations and cultures:

Generational Perspectives

Baby Boomers (born 1946-1964)
- Generally later adopters of digital technology
- May face challenges with digital literacy but often eager to learn
- Often use technology for practical purposes like staying connected with family
- May be more susceptible to online scams due to less familiarity with digital threats

Generation X (born 1965-1980)
- Straddle the pre-digital and digital eras
- Often comfortable with technology but may be more skeptical of its pervasiveness
- Tend to use social media platforms like Facebook to stay connected
- May struggle with balancing their own digital use and their children's screen time

Millennials (born 1981-1996)
- First generation to grow up with the internet
- Heavy users of social media and mobile technology
- Often seek health and wellness information online
- May face challenges with digital addiction and work-life balance due to constant connectivity

Generation Z (born 1997-2012)
- True digital natives
- Highly proficient with technology but may struggle with face-to-face communication
- Often use multiple screens simultaneously
- May face increased mental health challenges related to social media use

Cultural Variations

Western Cultures
- Generally more individualistic approach to digital wellness
- Focus on personal productivity and self-improvement through technology
- Growing concern about data privacy and digital rights

Eastern Cultures
- Often more collectivist approach, considering family and community in digital use
- In some countries, higher rates of internet and gaming addiction
- Cultural values may influence technology adoption and usage patterns

Developing Countries
- Digital divide issues may impact access to technology and digital wellness resources
- Mobile technology often plays a crucial role in accessing information and services
- Cultural norms may influence how technology is perceived and used

Cross-Cultural Considerations

1. Language barriers: Digital wellness resources may not be equally available in all languages.

2. Cultural values: Some cultures may prioritize constant connectivity, while others value unplugging.

3. Digital literacy: Varies widely across cultures and generations, impacting ability to engage in digital wellness practices.

4. Government regulations: Different countries have varying laws regarding internet use, privacy, and censorship, affecting digital wellness approaches.

5. Technological infrastructure: Access to high-speed internet and advanced devices varies globally, influencing digital wellness practices.

Understanding these generational and cultural differences is crucial for developing effective digital wellness strategies that are inclusive and respectful of diverse perspectives. As our world becomes increasingly connected, bridging these gaps and promoting universal digital wellness principles becomes ever more important.

Chapter 2: The Physical Impact of Screen Time

The increasing prevalence of screens in our daily lives has brought about significant physical health concerns. This chapter delves into the various ways excessive screen time can affect our bodies, from our eyes to our cardiovascular system.

Eye Strain and Vision Problems

Prolonged screen use can lead to a condition known as digital eye strain or computer vision syndrome. Symptoms include:

- Dry, irritated eyes
- Blurred vision
- Headaches
- Neck and shoulder pain

Research has shown that nearsightedness (myopia) has increased from 25% to 41.6% in the U.S. over the last 30 years, potentially linked to increased screen time and insufficient outdoor light exposure.

To mitigate these effects, eye care professionals recommend the 20-20-20 rule: every 20 minutes, take a 20-second break to look at something 20 feet away.

Musculoskeletal Issues

Poor posture while using devices can lead to various musculoskeletal problems:

- Neck pain ("tech neck")
- Back pain
- Repetitive strain injuries

Maintaining proper ergonomics is crucial. The optimal viewing angle for screens is around 15 degrees to decrease potential neck and back pain.

Sedentary Lifestyle and Obesity

Excessive screen time often correlates with a sedentary lifestyle, which can lead to:

- Increased risk of obesity
- Cardiovascular diseases
- Type 2 diabetes

Studies have consistently shown a strong association between screen time and obesity, especially among children and adolescents.

Cardiovascular Health

Prolonged sitting associated with screen use can adversely impact cardiovascular health:

- Increased risk of high blood pressure
- Poor stress regulation (high sympathetic arousal and cortisol dysregulation)
- Decreased HDL (good) cholesterol levels
- Insulin resistance.

Sleep Disruption

The blue light emitted by screens, particularly when used at night, can disrupt our sleep patterns:

- Suppression of melatonin production
- Difficulty falling asleep and staying asleep
- Overall poor sleep quality

These sleep disturbances can have cascading effects on both physical and mental health.

Other Physical Health Consequences

Additional physical impacts of excessive screen time include:

- Reduced bone density
- Increased risk of certain cancers associated with sedentary behavior
- Potential for repetitive stress injuries like carpal tunnel syndrome

Mitigating the Physical Impact

To reduce the negative physical effects of screen time:

1. Implement regular breaks and physical activity
2. Use proper ergonomics and posture when using devices
3. Utilize blue light filters, especially in the evening
4. Create screen-free zones and times, particularly before bedtime
5. Encourage outdoor activities and face-to-face interactions

By understanding these physical impacts and taking proactive steps to mitigate them, we can work towards a healthier relationship with our screens and better overall physical well-being.

Eye strain and vision problems:

Based on the search results and our previous discussion, here's an in-depth look at eye strain and vision problems related to screen time:

Eye Strain and Vision Problems

Prolonged screen use can lead to a condition known as digital eye strain or computer vision syndrome. This condition, while not typically causing permanent damage, can result in significant discomfort and temporary vision issues.

Symptoms of Digital Eye Strain

1. Eye discomfort (dry, irritated eyes)
2. Blurred vision
3. Headaches
4. Neck and shoulder pain

Causes of Digital Eye Strain

1. Extended screen time: The average American worker spends at least seven hours in front of a screen daily.

2. Reduced blinking: When staring at screens, people blink about half as often as normal, leading to dry eyes.
3. Blue light exposure: Screens emit blue light, which can contribute to eye strain2.
4. Poor posture and ergonomics: Improper viewing angles and posture can exacerbate eye strain.

Long-Term Concerns

While most effects of digital eye strain are temporary, some research suggests potential long-term impacts:

1. Myopia (nearsightedness): There's growing concern about increased rates of myopia, especially among children.
2. Age-related macular degeneration (AMD): Some studies suggest a potential link between sustained blue light exposure and impaired retinal cells.

Prevention and Mitigation Strategies

1. The 20-20-20 rule: Every 20 minutes, take a 20-second break to look at something 20 feet away.
2. Proper lighting: Ensure the light level in the room is roughly equal to the screen brightness.
3. Ergonomic adjustments: Correct posture and screen positioning can reduce strain1.
4. Use of artificial tears: Applying artificial tears before extended screen use can prevent eye dryness.
5. Blue light filters: Consider using screen filters or glasses designed to reduce blue light exposure.
6. Regular eye exams: Address any underlying vision problems that could exacerbate digital eye strain.

Special Considerations for Children

Children may be more susceptible to the effects of excessive screen time:

1. Higher blue light absorption: Children's eyes may absorb more blue light than adult eyes.
2. Developing vision: Extended screen time may impact visual development in children.

3. Increased risk: Children using screens for extended periods are at higher risk of developing vision problems.

While screens are an integral part of modern life, understanding and mitigating the potential impacts on our eyes is crucial for maintaining good vision and overall eye health. By implementing these strategies and being mindful of our screen use, we can significantly reduce the risk of eye strain and related vision problems.

Blue light exposure and its effects:

Blue light exposure and its effects have become a significant topic of research and concern in our increasingly digital world. Here's an overview of blue light exposure and its various effects:

What is Blue Light?

Blue light is a high-energy visible light with wavelengths between 415 and 495 nanometers1. It's a part of the visible light spectrum, which includes:

- Red
- Orange
- Yellow
- Green
- Blue
- Indigo
- Violet

Blue light has shorter wavelengths and higher energy compared to other colors in the visible spectrum.

Sources of Blue Light

1. Sunlight (the largest natural source)
2. Digital screens (smartphones, tablets, computers, TVs)
3. LED lights
4. Fluorescent lights
5. Compact fluorescent light (CFL) bulbs1

Effects on Eye Health

1. Digital Eye Strain: Blue light can decrease contrast on screens, leading to digital eyestrain. Symptoms include sore or irritated eyes and difficulty focusing.

2. Retinal Damage: Continued exposure to blue light over time could potentially lead to damaged retinal cells, which may cause vision problems like age-related macular degeneration.

3. Increased Risk of Cataracts: Some studies suggest that blue light exposure might increase the risk of cataracts.

Effects on Sleep

1. Circadian Rhythm Disruption: Blue light exposure, especially at night, can disrupt the body's natural wake and sleep cycle.

2. Melatonin Suppression: Blue light can suppress the release of melatonin, the hormone responsible for making us feel drowsy. Studies show that even 2 hours of exposure to blue light at night can significantly slow or stop melatonin release.

Potential Long-Term Health Impacts

1. Cancer Risk: Some studies have linked nighttime light exposure (including blue light) to an increased risk of certain cancers, particularly in night shift workers.

2. Obesity and Metabolic Disorders: Disruption of circadian rhythms due to blue light exposure may contribute to these conditions.

3. Mental Health: While nighttime exposure to blue light has been linked to depressive symptoms in animal studies, daytime exposure may have positive effects and has been used to treat seasonal affective disorder (SAD).

Protective Measures

1. Reduce screen time, especially before bedtime
2. Use blue light filters on digital devices
3. Wear computer glasses with yellow-tinted lenses

4. Use anti-reflective lenses
5. Increase exposure to natural daylight
6. Consider blue light-filtering intraocular lenses after cataract surgery.

While blue light is essential for regulating our circadian rhythms and has some health benefits, excessive exposure, particularly from artificial sources and at night, can have negative impacts. As research continues, it's important to be mindful of our blue light exposure and take steps to mitigate potential risks.

Musculoskeletal issues:

Based on the search results and our previous discussion, here's an overview of musculoskeletal issues related to screen time:

Musculoskeletal Issues

Prolonged screen use and associated sedentary behavior can lead to various musculoskeletal problems, particularly affecting the neck, back, and upper limbs.

Common Musculoskeletal Issues

1. Neck Pain ("Tech Neck")
   - Caused by looking down at screens for extended periods
   - Can lead to strain on neck muscles and ligaments
   - May result in decreased range of motion and stiffness

2. Back Pain
   - Lower back pain is particularly common
   - Associated with poor posture during screen use
   - Can lead to changes in lumbar lordosis and thoracolumbar kyphosis

3. Shoulder Pain
   - Often related to hunched posture while using devices
   - Can cause muscle imbalances and tension

4. Repetitive Strain Injuries
   - Including conditions like carpal tunnel syndrome
   - Often affects wrists and hands due to repetitive movements

Risk Factors

1. Duration of Screen Time
   - Screen times greater than 4 hours are associated with increased musculoskeletal pain
   - Risk of low back pain increases by 8.2% for each 1-hour of daily computer use

2. Poor Ergonomics
   - Improper positioning of screens, keyboards, and seating
   - Lack of ergonomic adjustments in workstations

3. Sedentary Behavior
   - Prolonged sitting associated with screen use
   - Lack of physical activity and movement

4. Age and Development
   - Adolescents are particularly vulnerable due to developing musculoskeletal systems

Impact on Different Body Regions

1. Upper Quadrant Musculoskeletal Pain (UQMP)
   - Affects neck, shoulders, and upper back
   - Common in adolescents due to screen-based activities

2. Spinal Pain
   - Includes neck, mid-back, and lower back pain
   - Prevalence increases with screen time and physical inactivity

3. Thoracolumbar Region
   - Changes in spinal curvature associated with excessive screen use

Prevention and Mitigation Strategies

1. Ergonomic Interventions
   - Adjusting chair and desk height, screen position, and keyboard placement
   - Using ergonomic accessories like supportive chairs and standing desks

2. Regular Breaks
   - Implementing the 20-20-20 rule (every 20 minutes, take a 20-second break to look at something 20 feet away)
   - Taking frequent movement breaks

3. Physical Activity
   - Engaging in regular exercise to counteract the effects of sedentary behavior
   - Incorporating stretching and strengthening exercises

4. Posture Awareness
   - Education on maintaining proper posture during screen use
   - Using posture-correcting devices or reminders

5. Screen Time Limits
   - Setting and adhering to reasonable limits on daily screen time
   - Encouraging alternative activities

By understanding these musculoskeletal issues and implementing preventive strategies, individuals can reduce the risk of developing screen-related musculoskeletal problems and maintain better overall physical health.

Carpal tunnel syndrome and repetitive strain injuries:

Carpal Tunnel Syndrome (CTS) and repetitive strain injuries (RSIs) are common conditions that can arise from prolonged and repetitive use of computers and other digital devices. Understanding these conditions is crucial for preventing and managing their symptoms effectively.

Carpal Tunnel Syndrome

What is Carpal Tunnel Syndrome?

Carpal Tunnel Syndrome is a condition caused by pressure on the median nerve as it passes through the carpal tunnel in the wrist. This narrow passageway is formed by the carpal bones and the transverse carpal ligament. The median nerve controls movement and sensation in the thumb and first three fingers, excluding the little finger.

Symptoms of Carpal Tunnel Syndrome

- Numbness and tingling in the thumb, index, middle, and ring fingers
- Weakness in the hand, leading to difficulty gripping objects
- Pain that may extend from the wrist up the arm
- Symptoms often worsen at night and may wake individuals from sleep

Causes and Risk Factors

- Repetitive hand movements, such as typing or using a mouse
- Anatomical factors, like a smaller carpal tunnel
- Health conditions such as diabetes, rheumatoid arthritis, and hypothyroidism
- Hormonal changes, particularly during pregnancy
- Obesity and age, with increased prevalence in individuals over 40

Diagnosis and Treatment

Diagnosis typically involves a physical examination and may include nerve conduction studies. Treatment options include:

- Conservative Treatments: Wrist splinting, especially at night, and anti-inflammatory medications
- Ergonomic Adjustments: Modifying workstations to reduce strain on the wrist
- Surgery: Carpal tunnel release surgery may be necessary if symptoms persist despite conservative measures

Repetitive Strain Injuries

What are Repetitive Strain Injuries?

RSIs refer to a range of conditions caused by repetitive movements and overuse of certain body parts, particularly affecting muscles, tendons, and nerves. These injuries are common in people who perform repetitive tasks, such as typing or using a mouse.

Common Types of RSIs

- Tendonitis: Inflammation of the tendons
- Bursitis: Inflammation of the fluid-filled sacs that cushion joints

- Epicondylitis: Inflammation of the tendons attached to the elbow (e.g., tennis elbow)

Symptoms of RSIs

- Pain and tenderness in the affected area
- Stiffness and restricted movement
- Numbness or tingling sensations
- Weakness in the hands or arms

Prevention and Management

- Ergonomic Workstations: Ensure proper alignment and support for wrists and arms
- Regular Breaks: Take frequent breaks to rest and stretch muscles
- Exercise and Stretching: Incorporate exercises to strengthen muscles and improve flexibility
- Proper Technique: Use correct posture and techniques when performing repetitive tasks

Understanding and addressing the risk factors for Carpal Tunnel Syndrome and repetitive strain injuries is essential for maintaining musculoskeletal health in the digital age. By implementing ergonomic practices and taking preventive measures, individuals can reduce the likelihood of developing these conditions and manage symptoms effectively if they arise.

Sleep disruption and circadian rhythm effects:

Sleep disruption and circadian rhythm effects are significant concerns related to blue light exposure, especially from digital screens. Here's an overview of these effects:

Sleep Disruption

1. Melatonin Suppression
   - Blue light exposure, particularly in the evening, suppresses the production of melatonin, the hormone responsible for regulating sleep-wake cycles.
   - This suppression can make it harder to fall asleep and reduce overall sleep quality.

2. Delayed Sleep Onset
   - Exposure to blue light before bedtime can increase sleep latency, meaning it takes longer to fall asleep.

- Studies have found that sleep latency can be increased in about half of the cases examined.

3. Reduced Sleep Quality
   - Some studies indicate that blue light exposure can decrease sleep quality.
   - However, the evidence is mixed, with about one-fifth of studies finding decreased sleep quality.

4. Decreased Sleep Duration
   - Blue light exposure has been associated with shorter sleep duration in about one-third of studies.

5. Reduced Sleep Efficiency
   - Sleep efficiency, which measures the proportion of time in bed actually spent sleeping, can be decreased by blue light exposure.

Circadian Rhythm Effects

1. Disruption of Natural Cycles
   - Blue light plays a crucial role in regulating circadian rhythms, our internal 24-hour cycles.
   - Exposure to blue light, especially at night, can trick the brain into thinking it's still daytime, disrupting these natural cycles.

2. Alertness and Performance
   - During the day, blue light exposure can improve alertness, attention, and performance.
   - However, this same effect at night can interfere with the body's natural preparation for sleep.

3. Physiological Changes
   - Blue light exposure can elevate body temperature and heart rate, which are typically lowered in preparation for sleep.

4. Shift in Circadian Timing
   - Chronic exposure to blue light at night can lead to a shift in circadian timing, potentially causing long-term sleep disorders.

5. Metabolic and Mental Health Impacts
  - Misalignment of circadian rhythms due to blue light exposure has been linked to metabolic disorders and mental health conditions like depression.

 Mitigating Strategies

1. Screen Curfews: Setting a specific time to stop using screens before bed.
2. Blue Light Filters: Using built-in night modes or blue light filtering apps on devices.
3. Dimming Screens: Reducing screen brightness in the evening.
4. Red Light at Night: Using dim red lights for nighttime illumination, as red light has the least effect on circadian rhythms.
5. Limiting Overall Screen Time: Especially in the hours leading up to bedtime.

While the effects of blue light on sleep and circadian rhythms are significant, it's worth noting that recent research suggests that blue light may not be uniquely disruptive compared to other types of light5. However, reducing overall light exposure, particularly from screens, in the evening remains a prudent approach for maintaining healthy sleep patterns.

Sedentary lifestyle consequences:

Based on the search results, here's an overview of the consequences of a sedentary lifestyle:

 Physical Consequences

1. Cardiovascular Disease
  - Increased risk of heart disease and stroke
  - Elevated blood pressure
  - Impaired blood circulation

2. Metabolic Disorders
  - Higher risk of type 2 diabetes
  - Insulin resistance
  - Metabolic syndrome
  - Obesity and weight gain

3. Musculoskeletal Issues

- Muscle weakness and imbalances
- Lower back pain and neck pain
- Poor spinal alignment
- Increased risk of osteoporosis and fractures
- Reduced bone density

4. Cancer Risk
  - Increased risk of certain cancers, including breast, colon, colorectal, endometrial, and ovarian cancer

5. Reduced Physical Fitness
  - Decreased cardiovascular endurance
  - Lower muscle strength and flexibility

Mental Health Implications

1. Cognitive Decline
  - Reduced brain function, particularly in areas related to memory and attention

2. Mood Disorders
  - Increased risk of depression and anxiety
  - Disrupted release of endorphins, the body's natural mood enhancers

3. Sleep Issues
  - Poor sleep quality
  - Insomnia
  - Disrupted circadian rhythms

Other Health Risks

1. Increased All-Cause Mortality
  - Higher risk of premature death, comparable to risks posed by obesity and smoking

2. Impaired Body Functions
  - Reduced lipoprotein lipase activity
  - Altered insulin-like growth factor axis
  - Changes in sex hormone levels
  - Elevated chronic inflammation

3. Varicose Veins
   - Increased risk, potentially leading to blood clots in rare cases

Long-term Health Impacts

- Chronic health conditions
- Reduced quality of life
- Increased healthcare costs
- Potential disability in later life

It's important to note that these consequences can occur even in individuals who meet recommended physical activity guidelines if they spend long periods being sedentary. Therefore, both reducing sedentary time and increasing physical activity are crucial for maintaining good health.

Chapter 3: Mental Health in the Digital World

Welcome to Chapter 3, where we delve into the fascinating and complex relationship between our digital lives and mental health. As we navigate this digital age, it's essential to understand how our mental well-being is intertwined with the technology we use every day. Let's explore the positive and negative impacts of digital technology on mental health and discover strategies for maintaining balance.

The Double-Edged Sword of Digital Technology

Digital technology is a double-edged sword when it comes to mental health. On one hand, it offers unprecedented access to information, support, and connection. On the other hand, it can contribute to stress, anxiety, and feelings of isolation if not managed mindfully.

Positive Impacts

1. Access to Resources: The internet provides a wealth of mental health resources, from online therapy platforms to educational content and support groups. This accessibility can be a lifeline for those seeking help.

2. Community and Connection: Social media and online communities can offer support and a sense of belonging, especially for individuals who may feel isolated in their offline lives.

3. Mental Health Apps: A growing number of apps offer tools for managing mental health, including meditation, mood tracking, and cognitive behavioral therapy exercises.

4. Awareness and Advocacy: Digital platforms have amplified voices advocating for mental health awareness, reducing stigma and encouraging open conversations.

Negative Impacts

1. Social Media Anxiety: While social media can connect us, it can also lead to feelings of inadequacy, jealousy, and anxiety. The curated nature of social media often presents an unrealistic picture of others' lives.

2. Information Overload: The constant stream of information can be overwhelming, leading to stress and difficulty focusing.

3. Cyberbullying and Harassment: Online platforms can sometimes become arenas for negative interactions, impacting mental well-being.

4. Digital Addiction: The compulsive use of digital devices can interfere with daily life, affecting sleep, productivity, and relationships.

Understanding the Impact on Different Age Groups

Children and Adolescents

- Young people are particularly vulnerable to the effects of digital technology on mental health. Excessive screen time can impact emotional regulation, social skills, and sleep.
- However, digital platforms can also provide valuable educational resources and opportunities for creative expression.

Adults

- For adults, digital technology can blur the lines between work and personal life, leading to stress and burnout.
- However, it also offers flexibility, remote work opportunities, and access to mental health support.

Seniors

- While some seniors may face challenges with digital literacy, technology can help combat loneliness and provide access to health information and services.

Strategies for Maintaining Digital Mental Health

1. Set Boundaries: Establish clear boundaries for digital use, such as tech-free times or zones, to prevent burnout and maintain focus.

2. Practice Mindfulness: Use mindfulness techniques to stay present and aware of your digital habits. Apps like Headspace and Calm can help integrate mindfulness into your routine.

3. Curate Your Digital Environment: Be intentional about who you follow and what content you consume. Unfollow accounts that trigger negative emotions and seek out positive, supportive communities.

4. Balance Screen Time: Monitor and limit screen time, especially before bed, to improve sleep quality and reduce stress.

5. Seek Professional Help: If digital technology is negatively impacting your mental health, consider seeking support from a mental health professional. Many therapists now offer online sessions.

The Future of Digital Mental Health

As technology continues to evolve, so too will its impact on mental health. Emerging technologies like virtual reality and AI hold promise for innovative mental health interventions. However, it's crucial to approach these advancements with caution and prioritize ethical considerations.

In conclusion, while digital technology presents challenges, it also offers opportunities for enhancing mental well-being. By understanding the potential impacts and implementing strategies for balance, we can harness the power of technology to support our mental health in the digital world. Remember, the key is mindful and intentional use, allowing technology to enhance rather than hinder our well-being. Let's continue this journey toward digital wellness together!

Social Media and Self-Esteem

Social media has become an integral part of modern life, especially for younger generations. While it offers many benefits, research suggests it can have significant impacts on self-esteem, particularly for adolescents and young adults.

Negative Impacts on Self-Esteem

1. Social Comparison
   - Social media encourages users to compare themselves to others, often leading to feelings of inadequacy.

- People tend to present idealized versions of their lives online, creating unrealistic standards for comparison.

2. Validation Seeking
  - The pursuit of likes, comments, and shares can tie self-worth to external validation.
  - Lack of engagement on posts can lead to feelings of rejection or invisibility.

3. Body Image Issues
  - Exposure to idealized body images and beauty standards can negatively impact body image, especially among young girls.
  - Filters and photo editing tools can create unrealistic expectations of appearance.

4. FOMO (Fear of Missing Out)
  - Constant exposure to others' activities can lead to anxiety and feelings of inadequacy.

5. Cyberbullying
  - Online harassment and negative interactions can severely impact self-esteem.

Positive Aspects

Despite these challenges, social media can also have positive effects on self-esteem:

1. Community Building
  - Connecting with like-minded individuals can boost confidence and sense of belonging.

2. Self-Expression
  - Social media platforms provide opportunities for creative expression and identity exploration.

3. Support Networks
  - Online communities can offer emotional support and encouragement.

Vulnerable Groups

Some groups are particularly susceptible to negative self-esteem impacts:

- Adolescents, especially girls aged 10-14
- Individuals with pre-existing mental health conditions

- People prone to social comparison

Strategies for Healthy Social Media Use

1. Mindful Consumption
   - Encourage critical thinking about content consumed on social media.
   - Remind users that social media often presents curated, idealized versions of life.

2. Set Boundaries
   - Limit daily social media use.
   - Create tech-free zones or times.

3. Diversify Activities
   - Encourage engagement in offline activities and in-person social interactions.

4. Curate Feeds
   - Follow accounts that inspire and uplift rather than those that trigger negative comparisons.

5. Practice Self-Awareness
   - Encourage reflection on how different social media interactions affect mood and self-esteem.

6. Seek Support
   - If social media is significantly impacting self-esteem, consider professional help.

In conclusion, while social media can have negative impacts on self-esteem, it's not inherently harmful. The key lies in fostering a healthy relationship with these platforms, promoting digital literacy, and maintaining a balanced lifestyle that doesn't revolve solely around online interactions. By understanding the potential pitfalls and implementing strategies for mindful use, individuals can harness the benefits of social media while protecting their self-esteem and overall mental well-being.

Anxiety and depression linked to digital use:

Based on the search results and our previous discussions, here's an overview of anxiety and depression linked to digital use:

 Anxiety and Depression Linked to Digital Use

The relationship between digital technology use and mental health, particularly anxiety and depression, is complex and multifaceted. Research has shown both positive and negative associations, with the impact varying based on individual factors, usage patterns, and the specific technologies involved.

Key Findings

1. Increased Prevalence
  - Studies have shown a correlation between increased digital media use and higher rates of anxiety and depression, especially among adolescents and young adults.
  - The SCAMP study revealed increases in depression and anxiety symptoms among adolescents during the COVID-19 pandemic, which coincided with increased digital technology use.

2. Gender Disparities
  - Females were found to be more likely to develop depression and anxiety related to digital use during the pandemic than males.
  - Some studies suggest that social media use may have a stronger negative association with mental health for girls compared to boys.

3. Specific Digital Activities
  - Social network site use and video gaming were associated with depression and anxiety, particularly during the pandemic.
  - Pre-pandemic high mobile phone use was linked to new incidents of depression during the pandemic.

4. Sleep Disruption
  - Insufficient sleep, often associated with late-night digital device use, was correlated with increased depression during the pandemic.

5. Moderate Use Benefits
   - Some research suggests that moderate digital media use may have few adverse effects and even some positive associations with well-being.

Mechanisms of Impact

1. Social Comparison and FOMO
   - Social media use can lead to increased social comparison and fear of missing out (FOMO), contributing to anxiety and depressive symptoms.

2. Information Overload
   - Constant exposure to news and information, especially during stressful events like the pandemic, can increase anxiety levels.

3. Disrupted Sleep Patterns
   - Blue light exposure and late-night device use can disrupt sleep, which is closely linked to mental health.

4. Reduced Face-to-Face Interactions
   - Excessive digital use may reduce in-person social interactions, which are crucial for mental well-being.

5. Cyberbullying and Online Harassment
   - Negative online experiences can significantly impact mental health, particularly for vulnerable individuals.

Positive Aspects

1. Access to Support
   - Digital platforms can provide access to mental health resources, support communities, and professional help.

2. Connection During Isolation
   - During periods of physical isolation, digital technologies can help maintain social connections, potentially mitigating loneliness and depression.

3. Self-Expression and Identity Exploration
  - Digital platforms can offer opportunities for self-expression and identity exploration, which can be beneficial for mental health.

Considerations for Future Research

1. Causality vs. Correlation
  - Many studies show correlations between digital use and mental health issues, but establishing causal relationships remains challenging.

2. Individual Differences
  - The impact of digital use on mental health varies significantly between individuals, suggesting the need for more personalized research approaches.

3. Long-Term Effects
  - More longitudinal studies are needed to understand the long-term impacts of digital technology use on mental health.

4. Intervention Strategies
  - Research is ongoing to develop effective digital interventions for anxiety and depression, leveraging technology for mental health support.

In conclusion, while there is evidence linking digital use to anxiety and depression, the relationship is complex. The key lies in promoting balanced and mindful use of digital technologies, recognizing both their potential benefits and risks to mental health. Future research and interventions should focus on personalized approaches and leveraging digital tools for positive mental health outcomes.

Chapter 3: Information Overload and Cognitive Effects

In our digital age, we are constantly bombarded with information from multiple sources emails, social media, news alerts, and more. This deluge of information can lead to a phenomenon known as information overload, which has significant cognitive effects.

Understanding Information Overload

Information overload occurs when the volume of information exceeds our brain's capacity to process it effectively. This can result in difficulty making decisions, decreased ability to retain information, and increased stress and anxiety14. Historically, periods of rapid technological advancement have often coincided with increased reports of information overload, as new technologies introduce new streams of information at a faster pace5.

Cognitive Effects of Information Overload

1. Memory Impairment: Our working memory, which holds information temporarily for processing, is limited to about seven items at a time. When overloaded, it becomes less efficient, leading to difficulties in retaining and recalling information.

2. Decreased Focus and Attention: Constant interruptions from notifications and the need to multitask can erode our ability to concentrate on a single task. Studies show that it can take up to 24 minutes to regain focus after an interruption.

3. Decision-Making Difficulties: With too much information, we may struggle to discern what is important, leading to indecision or poor decision-making. This is sometimes referred to as the "paradox of choice," where more options make it harder to choose.

4. Increased Stress and Fatigue: The cognitive load from processing excessive information can lead to mental fatigue, irritability, and stress. Our brain's energy resources are depleted, affecting both our cognitive function and emotional well-being.

Strategies to Manage Information Overload

1. Prioritize Information: Use tools like the Eisenhower Matrix to categorize tasks by urgency and importance, helping to focus on what truly matters.

2. Limit Multitasking: Focus on one task at a time to improve productivity and reduce cognitive load. Multitasking can give the illusion of efficiency but often leads to decreased performance.

3. Filter and Organize Information: Use technology to filter emails and notifications, ensuring that only the most relevant information reaches you. Organizing information can help reduce the sense of being overwhelmed.

4. Set Boundaries: Allocate specific times for checking emails and social media, and turn off notifications during periods of focused work to minimize distractions.

5. Take Breaks: Regular breaks are essential for cognitive rest and recovery. Stepping away from screens can help refresh the mind and improve overall cognitive efficiency.

While information overload is a challenge in our connected world, understanding its cognitive effects can help us develop strategies to manage it effectively. By prioritizing information, limiting distractions, and focusing on one task at a time, we can mitigate the negative impacts of information overload and enhance our cognitive well-being. As we continue to navigate the digital landscape, being mindful of how we consume and process information will be key to maintaining mental clarity and productivity.

Digital addiction: signs and symptoms:

Based on the search results and our previous discussions, here's an overview of the signs and symptoms of digital addiction:

Digital Addiction: Signs and Symptoms

Digital addiction, also known as internet addiction, is characterized by excessive and compulsive use of digital devices and online activities that interfere with daily life. Here are the key signs and symptoms:

Behavioral Signs

1. Preoccupation with the Internet: Constantly thinking about online activities or anticipating the next online session.

2. Loss of Time Control: Spending more time online than intended, often losing track of time.

3. Failed Attempts to Cut Back: Unsuccessful efforts to reduce or control internet use.

4. Neglecting Responsibilities: Sacrificing work, school, or personal obligations due to excessive internet use.

5. Social Withdrawal: Preferring online interactions over real-life relationships.

6. Concealment: Lying about or hiding the extent of internet use from others.

7. Using the Internet as Escape: Turning to online activities to avoid problems or relieve negative moods.

Psychological Symptoms

1. Euphoria When Online: Experiencing a heightened sense of pleasure or excitement while using the internet.

2. Anxiety or Irritability When Offline: Feeling restless, moody, or depressed when unable to access the internet.

3. Increased Tolerance: Needing to spend more time online to achieve satisfaction.

4. Withdrawal Symptoms: Experiencing unpleasant feelings when internet use is limited or stopped.

Physical Symptoms

1. Sleep Disturbances: Difficulty falling asleep, staying asleep, or maintaining a regular sleep schedule.

2. Fatigue: Chronic tiredness due to late-night internet use and disrupted sleep patterns.

3. Physical Discomfort: Muscle aches, back pain, or eye strain from prolonged sedentary behavior and screen time.

4. Neglect of Personal Hygiene: Reduced attention to self-care and grooming.

Types of Digital Addiction

Digital addiction can manifest in various forms, including:

- Social media addiction
- Online gaming addiction
- Cybersex or online pornography addiction
- Information overload (compulsive web surfing)
- Online gambling addiction
- Online shopping addiction4

It's important to note that digital addiction is not yet formally recognized as a clinical disorder in the DSM-5. However, these signs and symptoms are widely acknowledged by researchers and mental health professionals as indicators of problematic internet use. If you or someone you know is experiencing several of these signs, it may be beneficial to seek professional help or support in managing digital use.

Positive psychology and digital well-being:

Based on the search results and our previous discussions, here's an overview of positive psychology and digital well-being:

Positive Psychology and Digital Well-being

Positive psychology, which focuses on cultivating human strengths and virtues, has increasingly been applied to the digital realm to promote digital well-being. This approach aims to leverage technology to enhance psychological flourishing rather than merely mitigating its negative impacts.

Key Concepts

1. Strengths-Based Approach: Positive psychology emphasizes identifying and developing individual strengths. In the digital context, this involves using technology in ways that align with and enhance personal strengths.

2. Flow and Engagement: The concept of "flow" - a state of complete absorption in an activity - can be applied to digital experiences to promote engagement and well-being.

3. Positive Relationships: Technology can be used to foster and maintain positive relationships, a key component of well-being.

4. Meaning and Purpose: Digital tools can be leveraged to help individuals find and pursue meaningful goals and activities.

Applications in Digital Well-being

1. Mindfulness Apps: Many digital interventions incorporate mindfulness practices, which align with positive psychology principles of present-moment awareness and emotional regulation.

2. Gratitude Journaling: Digital platforms that encourage gratitude journaling can boost positive emotions and overall well-being.

3. Strength-Based Social Media Use: Encouraging users to share and celebrate their strengths and accomplishments on social media, rather than engaging in social comparison.

4. Goal-Setting and Achievement Apps: Digital tools that help users set, track, and achieve personal goals can enhance self-efficacy and life satisfaction.

5. Positive Gaming: Designing games that promote prosocial behavior, problem-solving skills, and personal growth.

Research Findings

While research on positive psychology interventions in digital contexts is still emerging, some studies have shown promising results:

- Digital interventions based on mindfulness, acceptance, commitment, and compassion have shown significant positive effects on mental well-being in the general population.

- Positive psychology interventions delivered via smartphone apps have demonstrated potential in improving well-being and reducing depressive symptoms.

- However, the effectiveness of these interventions can vary, and more research is needed to understand the long-term impacts and optimal delivery methods.

Challenges and Considerations

1. Adherence: As with other digital interventions, maintaining user engagement and adherence can be challenging.

2. Personalization: Positive psychology interventions may need to be tailored to individual needs and preferences for maximum effectiveness.

3. Balancing Online and Offline Experiences: While digital tools can enhance well-being, it's crucial to maintain a balance with offline activities and relationships.

4. Ethical Considerations: Ensuring that positive psychology principles are applied ethically in digital contexts, without manipulating users or oversimplifying complex psychological processes.

In conclusion, positive psychology offers a promising framework for promoting digital well-being by focusing on strengths, positive experiences, and personal growth. As research in this area continues to evolve, it has the potential to shape more effective and engaging digital interventions for mental health and well-being.

Chapter 4: Relationships and Communication:

Based on the search results and our previous discussions, here's an overview for Chapter 4 on Relationships and Communication:

Chapter 4: Relationships and Communication

Introduction:
Communication is fundamental to building and maintaining relationships, both personal and professional. This chapter explores how effective communication can strengthen relationships and how poor communication can damage them.

Key Topics:

1. The Importance of Communication in Relationships
- Communication as the foundation for understanding and connection
- How communication styles impact relationship dynamics

2. Building Trust Through Communication
- The role of honesty and transparency in fostering trust
- Active listening and empathy as trust-building tools
- Providing and receiving feedback constructively

3. Supportive Communication
- Principles of supportive communication (e.g., being descriptive rather than evaluative)
- How to communicate during difficult conversations or conflicts
- Balancing assertiveness with sensitivity

4. Nonverbal Communication in Relationships
- The impact of body language, facial expressions, and tone of voice
- Cultural differences in nonverbal communication

5. Technology and Relationship Communication
- Pros and cons of digital communication in relationships
- Best practices for using technology to enhance rather than hinder relationships

6. Overcoming Communication Barriers
- Identifying common barriers (e.g., assumptions, defensiveness)
- Strategies for improving communication skills

7. Communication in Different Types of Relationships
- Professional relationships (colleagues, clients, supervisors)
- Personal relationships (friends, family, romantic partners)
- Adapting communication styles for different relationship contexts

8. Conflict Resolution Through Effective Communication
- Techniques for addressing disagreements constructively
- The importance of timing and approach in difficult conversations

9. Building and Maintaining Relationships
- Strategies for initiating new relationships
- Nurturing existing relationships through consistent, positive communication

10. Self-Reflection and Improvement
- Assessing one's own communication strengths and weaknesses
- Setting goals for improving relationship communication skills

Effective communication is essential for building strong, lasting relationships. By understanding the principles of supportive communication, recognizing the impact of nonverbal cues, and continuously working to improve our communication skills, we can enhance our personal and professional relationships.

Exercises:
- Role-playing scenarios to practice supportive communication
- Journaling about personal communication challenges and successes
- Group discussions on technology's impact on modern relationships

This chapter aims to provide a comprehensive understanding of how communication shapes our relationships and offers practical strategies for improving interpersonal connections through better communication.

The impact of digital devices on personal relationships:

The impact of digital devices on personal relationships is multifaceted, with both positive and negative effects. Here is an overview based on the provided search results:

Positive Impacts

1. Enhanced Communication: Digital devices allow for instant communication through texts, calls, and video chats, making it easier to stay connected with loved ones across distances.

2. Support and Connection: Technology can help maintain relationships by providing platforms for sharing experiences and offering support, especially in long-distance relationships.

3. Shared Experiences: Digital devices enable shared experiences, such as watching movies together online or playing games, which can strengthen bonds.

Negative Impacts

1. Decreased Face-to-Face Interaction: Over-reliance on digital communication can lead to a reduction in face-to-face interactions, which are crucial for emotional intimacy and understanding.

2. Authenticity Challenges: Online interactions may not always reflect true emotions or intentions, leading to misunderstandings and misinterpretations due to the absence of nonverbal cues.

3. Fear of missing out (FOMO): Social media platforms often highlight idealized versions of life, leading to comparisons and feelings of inadequacy, which can strain relationships.

4. Reduced Empathy and Social Skills: Excessive use of digital devices can result in decreased empathy and weakened social skills, contributing to feelings of loneliness.

5. Distraction from Real-Life Connections: Digital devices can distract individuals from engaging fully in real-life interactions, impacting the quality of time spent with partners, family, and friends.

6. Privacy Concerns: Sharing devices and digital platforms can lead to privacy issues, which may cause tension in relationships.

Strategies for Balancing Digital and Real-Life Interactions

1. Set Boundaries: Establish clear boundaries for technology use during real-life interactions to ensure focused and meaningful connections.

2. Prioritize Face-to-Face Time: Make an effort to engage in face-to-face interactions whenever possible to strengthen emotional bonds.

3. Limit Social Media Use: Be mindful of the time spent on social media and focus on building genuine connections in the real world.

4. Engage in Shared Activities: Participate in activities that foster bonding and shared experiences, such as hobbies or outings together.

5. Practice Active Listening: During interactions, practice active listening to understand emotions and needs, showing empathy and presence.

6. Plan Tech-Free Days: Designate specific days as tech-free to prioritize spending quality time with loved ones without digital distractions.

In conclusion, while digital devices have transformed the way we connect, maintaining a balance between virtual and real-life interactions is essential for nurturing healthy and fulfilling relationships. By setting boundaries and prioritizing face-to-face connections, we can harness the benefits of technology while preserving the depth and authenticity of our personal relationships.

Online Communication

Advantages:
1. Convenience and accessibility: Available 24/7 with global reach
2. Speed: Allows for instant communication across distances
3. Flexibility: Various tools and formats available (email, chat, video calls, etc.)
4. Efficiency: Can communicate with multiple people simultaneously
5. Record-keeping: Easy to save and reference past communications

Disadvantages:
1. Lack of nonverbal cues: Can lead to misunderstandings
2. Potential for misinterpretation: Tone and context can be lost in text
3. Privacy and security concerns: Risk of cyberattacks or data breaches
4. Information overload: Can cause stress and distraction
5. Reduced empathy: May hinder development of deep connections

Offline Communication

Advantages:
1. Personal touch: Builds stronger rapport and trust
2. Nonverbal cues: Facial expressions, tone, and body language enhance understanding
3. Immediate feedback: Allows for real-time clarification and discussion
4. Builds deeper connections: Fosters empathy and emotional bonds
5. Better for complex or sensitive topics: Allows for nuanced discussion

Disadvantages:
1. Time and place restrictions: Requires physical presence
2. Can be time-consuming: Meetings and travel take more time
3. Limited reach: Restricted to those physically present
4. Lack of record: Unless recorded, no automatic documentation
5. Potential for interruptions or distractions in the physical environment

Balancing Online and Offline Communication

1. Choose the right mode based on the purpose and audience
2. Use online for routine and urgent matters, offline for complex or sensitive issues
3. Set clear expectations for online communication (availability, response time, etc.)
4. Make time for regular face-to-face meetings to build relationships
5. Enhance both online and offline communication skills
6. Be mindful of the quantity and quality of both types of communication

In conclusion, both online and offline communication have their place in modern work
and personal life. The key is to understand the strengths and weaknesses of each and use
them appropriately based on the situation and goals of the communication.

Digital etiquette and boundaries:

Based on the search results and our previous discussions, here's an overview of digital etiquette and boundaries:

Digital Etiquette (Netiquette)

Digital etiquette, also known as netiquette, refers to the set of guidelines for acceptable behavior in online communication. Key principles include:

1. Treat others with respect: Apply the "golden rule" - treat others as you would like to be treated online.

2. Be mindful of tone: Without face-to-face cues, written communication can be easily misinterpreted. Be clear and considerate in your language.

3. Think before you post: Once something is online, it can be difficult or impossible to retract. Consider the potential impact of your words.

4. Respect privacy: Don't share personal information about others without their consent.

5. Use appropriate language: Avoid offensive language, all caps (perceived as shouting), and excessive use of exclamation points.

6. Be concise: Keep messages focused and on-topic, especially in professional contexts.

7. Respond in a timely manner: While constant availability isn't expected, try to respond within a reasonable timeframe.

Setting Digital Boundaries

Establishing clear boundaries in digital communication is crucial for maintaining healthy relationships and work-life balance:

1. Establish "tech-free" times and zones: Designate specific times or areas where digital devices are not used, such as during meals or in bedrooms.

2. Communicate your availability: Let others know when you're available for digital communication and when you're not.

3. Limit notifications: Turn off non-essential notifications to reduce distractions and control when you engage with digital communication.

4. Separate work and personal accounts: Use different accounts or devices for work and personal communication to maintain a clear division.

5. Be clear about expectations: In professional settings, establish clear guidelines for response times and appropriate communication channels.

6. Respect others' boundaries: Be mindful of others' time and privacy, and don't expect immediate responses.

7. Practice digital detox: Regularly take breaks from digital devices to recharge and focus on in-person interactions.

Implementing Digital Etiquette and Boundaries

1. Lead by example: Model good digital etiquette and boundary-setting for others, especially children and colleagues.

2. Educate: Teach digital etiquette and the importance of boundaries, particularly in schools and workplaces.

3. Use tools and settings: Utilize built-in features on devices and platforms to help maintain boundaries, such as "Do Not Disturb" modes or screen time limits.

4. Regular review: Periodically assess your digital habits and adjust your boundaries as needed.

5. Open communication: Discuss digital etiquette and boundaries with family, friends, and colleagues to ensure mutual understanding and respect.

By adhering to these principles of digital etiquette and setting clear boundaries, we can create a more respectful and balanced digital environment, enhancing our online interactions and overall well-being.

Building meaningful connections in a digital world:

Based on the search results and our previous discussions, here's an overview of building meaningful connections in a digital world:

The Importance of Meaningful Connections

In today's digital age, cultivating genuine relationships is crucial for our well-being and happiness. Meaningful connections provide:

- Emotional support
- Validation
- A sense of belonging
- Increased resilience
- Improved mental and emotional health

Key Components of Meaningful Digital Relationships

1. Authenticity: Be true to yourself and express thoughts and feelings honestly.

2. Empathy: Understand and share others' feelings, even without nonverbal cues.

3. Active Listening: Fully engage in conversations, focusing on what others are saying.

4. Reciprocity: Contribute to the relationship's growth through mutual exchange.

5. Shared Values and Interests: Find common ground to foster connection and belonging.

Strategies for Building Meaningful Connections Online

1. Be Genuine: Share your thoughts, feelings, and experiences openly and honestly.

2. Practice Empathy: Put yourself in others' shoes and respond with kindness.

3. Cultivate Active Listening: Ask questions and show genuine interest in others' thoughts.

4. Be Reciprocal: Offer support, encouragement, and kindness to others.

5. Seek Common Ground: Find shared values, interests, and experiences.

6. Prioritize Quality Time: Make conscious efforts to spend focused time with loved ones.

7. Express Appreciation: Use digital platforms to show gratitude, but also convey sentiments in person when possible.

8. Engage in Deep Conversations: Move beyond small talk to discuss meaningful topics.

Balancing Digital and In-Person Interactions

1. Set boundaries on screen time to improve communication quality.

2. Carve out dedicated time for face-to-face interactions.

3. Use technology intentionally to enhance rather than replace in-person connections.

4. Participate in digital detoxes to fully immerse in surroundings and create valuable face-to-face interactions.

5. Rediscover hobbies and activities that bring joy outside the digital world.

Leveraging Technology for Positive Connections

1. Use social media platforms to share experiences and maintain long-distance relationships.

2. Utilize video conferencing for face-to-face conversations when in-person meetings aren't possible.

3. Join online communities centered around shared interests to foster connections.

4. Use technology as a tool for education and personal growth, enhancing your ability to connect with others.

By implementing these strategies and maintaining a balance between digital and in-person interactions, we can build and nurture meaningful connections in our increasingly digital world. Remember that while technology offers new ways to connect, it should complement rather than replace the depth and quality of in-person relationships.

Chapter 5: The Blue Light Challenge

Understanding Blue Light
Blue light is a type of high-energy visible light that is part of the visible light spectrum. It is naturally present in sunlight and plays a crucial role in regulating our circadian rhythms, which help control our sleep-wake cycles. However, with the increasing use of digital devices, artificial blue light exposure has become a significant concern.

Blue Light from Screens and Monitors
Digital devices such as smartphones, tablets, computers, and LED TVs emit blue light. The LED backlights used in these screens are particularly rich in blue light wavelengths. While beneficial during the day for boosting attention and mood, excessive exposure to blue light, especially in the evening, can disrupt sleep patterns and lead to digital eye strain.

Reducing Blue Light Exposure
To mitigate the effects of blue light exposure, consider the following strategies:
- Use blue light filtering apps or built-in settings on devices.
- Wear blue light blocking glasses.
- Install physical screen filters.
- Limit screen time, particularly before bedtime.
- Increase exposure to natural light during the day.
- Use warm, dim lighting in the evening.

Adjusting Blue Light Settings on Different Devices
Most modern devices offer settings to reduce blue light exposure:
- iOS Devices: Use the Night Shift feature to adjust screen colors to warmer tones.
- Android Devices: Activate Night Light or Blue Light Filter options.
- Windows 10: Enable Night Light to reduce blue light emission.
- MacOS: Use Night Shift to adjust display colors.
- Smart TVs: Look for Eye Care or Comfort View settings to reduce blue light.

Best Practices for Blue Light Management
- Follow the 20-20-20 rule: Every 20 minutes, look at something 20 feet away for 20 seconds.
- Position screens at arm's length and slightly below eye level.
- Adjust screen brightness to match ambient lighting.

- Take regular breaks from screen use.
- Create a "screen-free" bedroom environment.
- Expose yourself to plenty of natural light during the day.
- Consider using warm, dim lighting in the evening.

Measuring Blue Light Exposure
While precise measurement of blue light exposure typically requires specialized equipment, you can estimate your exposure by:
- Using smartphone apps designed to measure light intensity and spectrum.
- Tracking screen time using built-in device features or third-party apps.
- Being aware of the types of lighting in your environment (LED, fluorescent, incandescent).
- Considering the time of day and duration of exposure to different light sources.

By understanding and managing blue light exposure, we can protect our eyes, improve sleep quality, and maintain overall well-being in our increasingly digital world.

Understanding blue light:

Blue light is a high-energy visible light with wavelengths between approximately 380 and 500 nanometers. It's part of the visible light spectrum, which includes:

- Red
- Orange
- Yellow
- Green
- Blue
- Indigo
- Violet

Key points about blue light:

1. It has shorter wavelengths and higher energy compared to other colors in the visible spectrum.

2. Blue light is naturally present in sunlight, which is the largest source of blue light exposure.

3. Artificial sources of blue light include:
   - Digital screens (smartphones, tablets, computers, TVs)
   - LED lights
   - Fluorescent lights
   - Compact fluorescent light (CFL) bulbs

4. The human eye is not very effective at blocking blue light, so more of it passes through to the retina compared to other types of light.

5. Blue light plays an important role in regulating circadian rhythms, boosting alertness, and elevating mood during daytime hours.

6. However, exposure to blue light, especially from artificial sources at night, can disrupt sleep patterns by suppressing melatonin production.

7. There are concerns about potential long-term effects of blue light exposure on eye health, though more research is needed. Some studies suggest it may contribute to digital eye strain and potentially increase the risk of macular degeneration.

8. Children's eyes may be more susceptible to blue light as they don't filter it as effectively as adult eyes.

9. Blue light scatters more easily in the atmosphere, which is why the sky appears blue.

Understanding blue light and its sources helps in developing strategies to manage exposure and mitigate potential negative effects, especially from digital devices and artificial lighting.

Blue light from screens and monitors:

Digital screens, including those on smartphones, tablets, computers, and LED TVs, are significant sources of blue light. This type of light is part of the visible spectrum and is characterized by its short wavelength and high energy. While blue light is naturally present in sunlight and plays a role in regulating our circadian rhythms, the artificial blue light emitted by digital devices has raised concerns due to its potential impact on eye health and sleep.

Eye Health Concerns

1. Digital Eye Strain: Prolonged exposure to blue light from screens can lead to digital eye strain, characterized by symptoms such as dry eyes, blurred vision, and headaches. This condition is often referred to as computer vision syndrome.

2. Potential Retinal Damage: There is ongoing research into whether long-term exposure to blue light from screens could contribute to retinal damage and increase the risk of conditions like age-related macular degeneration. While the evidence is not yet conclusive, it is a topic of concern among eye health professionals.

Sleep Disruption

Blue light exposure, particularly in the evening, can interfere with the body's natural sleep-wake cycle by suppressing the production of melatonin, a hormone that signals the body to prepare for sleep. This disruption can lead to difficulties falling asleep and reduced sleep quality. Many people use electronic devices close to bedtime, which can exacerbate these effects.

Mitigation Strategies

To reduce the potential negative impacts of blue light from screens, consider the following strategies:

- Use Blue Light Filters: Many devices offer built-in settings or apps that reduce blue light emission by adjusting the screen to warmer tones, often referred to as "night mode" or "night shift."

- Screen Time Management: Reducing overall screen time, especially before bed, can help minimize blue light exposure.

- Protective Eyewear: Blue light blocking glasses are available and can be worn while using digital devices to reduce eye strain.

- Environmental Adjustments: Use ambient lighting that minimizes glare and complements screen use, and consider screen protectors that filter blue light.

Understanding the effects of blue light from screens and taking proactive steps to manage exposure can help mitigate potential risks to eye health and improve sleep quality.

Reducing blue light exposure:

Based on the search results, here are some key strategies for reducing blue light exposure:

1. Limit screen time:
   - Take regular breaks from screens using the 20-20-20 rule: Every 20 minutes, look at something 20 feet away for 20 seconds.
   - Try to stop using devices at least 3 hours before bedtime.

2. Adjust device settings:
   - Use built-in blue light filter settings like Night Shift (iOS/macOS), Night Light (Windows), or Night Mode (Android).
   - Reduce screen brightness, especially in the evening.
   - Increase contrast on screens.

3. Use blue light filtering apps:
   - Install apps like f.lux on computers to automatically adjust screen color temperature.

4. Wear blue light blocking glasses:
   - Use computer glasses with yellow-tinted lenses during the day.
   - Use orange-tinted glasses in the evening for stronger blue light blocking.

5. Apply screen filters:
   - Add physical blue light filtering screens to devices.

6. Modify your environment:
   - Use warm, dim lighting in the evening instead of bright blue-tinted lights.
   - Ensure ambient room lighting matches screen brightness to reduce eye strain.

7. Consider supplements:
   - Some studies suggest lutein and zeaxanthin supplements may help, but consult a doctor first.

8. Get natural light exposure:
   - Spend time outdoors during the day to help regulate your circadian rhythm.

9. Use alternative light sources:
   - For evening reading, use lamps that emit red or orange light rather than blue.

10. Practice good sleep hygiene:
    - Create a "screen-free" bedroom environment.
    - Establish a consistent sleep schedule.

Remember, the most effective approach is to implement a combination of these strategies as part of a long-term plan to manage blue light exposure.

Adjusting Blue Light Settings on Different Devices:

Managing blue light exposure is essential for maintaining eye health and improving sleep quality. Here's how to adjust blue light settings on various devices:

iPhone and iPad

1. Night Shift:
   - Go to Settings > Display & Brightness.
   - Tap on Night Shift.
   - You can choose to enable it manually or schedule it to turn on automatically.
   - Adjust the color temperature using the slider to make the display warmer.

2. Red Light Filter:
   - Go to Settings > Accessibility > Display & Text Size.
   - Scroll down to Color Filters and toggle it on.
   - Select Color Tint and adjust the Intensity slider to the maximum position for a red filter, which effectively blocks blue light.

3. Control Center Access:
   - Open the Control Center, press and hold the brightness icon, and tap the Night Shift button to toggle it on or off quickly.

Android Devices

1. Night Light or Blue Light Filter:
   - Go to Settings > Display.
   - Look for Night Light, Blue Light Filter, or Eye Comfort Shield.
   - Enable the feature and customize the schedule and intensity as desired.

2. Third-Party Apps:
   - If your device doesn't have built-in options, consider downloading apps like Blue Light Filter or sFilter to manage blue light exposure.

Windows 10 and 11

1. Night Light:
   - Go to Settings > System > Display.
   - Toggle the Night light switch to enable it.
   - Click on Night light settings to customize the schedule and color temperature.

Mac

1. Night Shift:
   - Go to System Preferences > Displays.
   - Click on the Night Shift tab.
   - Schedule Night Shift to turn on automatically or manually adjust the color temperature.

General Tips

- Screen Protectors: Consider using blue light blocking screen protectors for additional protection on laptops and mobile devices.

- Blue Light Glasses: Wearing blue light blocking glasses can help reduce exposure without needing to adjust device settings.

By adjusting these settings across your devices, you can effectively manage blue light exposure and promote better eye health and sleep quality.

Chapter 6: Productivity and Work-Life Balance:

Chapter 6: Productivity and Work-Life Balance

This chapter explores the interconnected concepts of productivity and work-life balance, examining how they impact both individual well-being and organizational success.

Understanding Productivity

Productivity is a key measure of economic efficiency and growth. It's typically defined as the amount of output produced per unit of input.

Key points on productivity:

1. Labor productivity is a common measure, calculated as output per worker or per hour worked.

2. Productivity growth is crucial for improving living standards and economic competitiveness.

3. The UK, like many developed economies, has experienced a "productivity puzzle" with stagnant productivity growth since the 2008 financial crisis.

4. Factors affecting productivity include technology, skills, management practices, and investment.

Work-Life Balance

Work-life balance refers to the equilibrium between one's work and personal life. It's increasingly recognized as important for both employee well-being and organizational performance.

Key aspects of work-life balance:

1. It involves managing time and energy between work responsibilities and personal/family life.

2. Technology has blurred the lines between work and personal time, creating new challenges.

3. Achieving balance can reduce stress, improve job satisfaction, and enhance overall quality of life.

4. Work-life balance needs vary across different demographics and life stages.

The Productivity-Balance Connection

There's a complex relationship between productivity and work-life balance:

1. Overwork can lead to burnout, reducing long-term productivity.

2. Good work-life balance can increase engagement and creativity, potentially boosting productivity.

3. Flexible work arrangements, when implemented effectively, can improve both balance and productivity.

4. Cultural differences affect perceptions and practices around work-life balance and productivity.

Strategies for Improving Productivity and Balance

1. Time management techniques (e.g., Pomodoro method, time-blocking)
2. Setting clear boundaries between work and personal time
3. Embracing technology mindfully to enhance efficiency without encroaching on personal time
4. Encouraging regular breaks and time off to prevent burnout
5. Implementing flexible work policies that suit both organizational and employee needs

Measuring Success

1. Productivity metrics (e.g., output per hour, revenue per employee)
2. Employee satisfaction and engagement surveys
3. Work-life balance indicators (e.g., overtime hours, use of vacation time)

4. Health and well-being measures (e.g., stress levels, absenteeism rates)

Future Trends

1. Increasing adoption of remote and hybrid work models
2. Growing emphasis on results-oriented work environments rather than time-based measures
3. Use of AI and automation to enhance productivity while freeing up human time
4. Greater focus on mental health and well-being in the workplace

By understanding and effectively managing the interplay between productivity and work-life balance, organizations can create environments that foster both high performance and employee satisfaction.

Digital distractions and focus:

Understanding Digital Distractions

Digital distractions refer to interruptions caused by electronic devices and online platforms that divert our attention from tasks at hand. Common types include:

- Social media notifications
- Email alerts
- App notifications
- Instant messaging
- Online advertisements
- Multimedia content
- Unplanned web browsing

These distractions can significantly impact focus, productivity, and overall well-being.

Impact of Digital Distractions

1. Decreased productivity and efficiency
2. Shortened attention spans
3. Disrupted sleep patterns due to blue light exposure
4. Reduced enjoyment of in-person activities
5. Lingering effects on focus even after device use

6. Potential for behavioral addiction to technology

Strategies to Manage Digital Distractions and Improve Focus

1. Manage notifications:
   - Turn off non-essential notifications
   - Customize settings for essential apps
   - Use "Do Not Disturb" modes

2. Create tech-free zones and times:
   - Designate areas where devices are not allowed
   - Set specific times for digital detox

3. Use focus-enhancing techniques:
   - Implement the Pomodoro technique (work in focused bursts)
   - Allow scheduled "distraction breaks"

4. Optimize device settings:
   - Use blue light filters, especially in the evening
   - Switch phone displays to black and white to reduce visual appeal

5. Practice mindful device use:
   - Be intentional about when and why you use devices
   - Regularly assess your digital habits

6. Improve your environment:
   - Keep devices out of sight when focusing
   - Create a dedicated, distraction-free workspace

7. Utilize focus-enhancing apps and tools:
   - Use website blockers during work hours
   - Try apps designed to improve concentration

8. Prioritize in-person interactions:
   - Be fully present during face-to-face conversations
   - Avoid device use during meals with others

9. Develop healthy sleep habits:
   - Avoid screens before bedtime
   - Use night mode settings on devices in the evening

By implementing these strategies, you can reduce the impact of digital distractions and improve your ability to focus on important tasks. Remember that managing digital distractions is an ongoing process that may require regular adjustment and self-reflection.

Time management in the digital age:

Based on the search results, here are key points about time management in the digital age:

1. Analyze your time use:
   - Conduct a SWOT analysis of your working time to identify opportunities, threats, strengths, and weaknesses.
   - Create a time budget by documenting activities every 15 minutes for several days to identify "time thieves" and inefficiencies.

2. Prioritize tasks:
   - Identify your most important tasks (MITs) and tackle them first.
   - Use techniques like time blocking to allocate specific periods for focused work, meetings, and breaks.

3. Manage digital distractions:
   - Turn off non-essential notifications.
   - Designate tech-free zones and times.
   - Set strict schedules for checking emails and social media.

4. Use technology effectively:
   - Utilize productivity apps and tools for task management and time tracking.
   - Automate repetitive tasks where possible.

5. Implement effective email strategies:
   - Schedule specific times to respond to emails.
   - Sort emails into urgency-based folders (e.g., "today," "this week," "this month").
   - For quick responses (under 3 minutes), deal with emails immediately; otherwise, save for dedicated email time.

6. Take regular breaks:
   - Use interruptions actively for stress relief and relaxation.
   - Take walks or do stretching exercises to refresh your mind.

7. Balance digital and face-to-face communication:
   - Know when to have in-person conversations instead of lengthy email chains.
   - Foster a culture of focus in the workplace by setting clear expectations about communication and availability.

8. Practice self-care and maintain work-life balance:
   - Prioritize activities that contribute to overall well-being.
   - Establish boundaries between work and personal life, especially when working from home.

9. Continuously improve:
   - Regularly review and adjust your time management strategies.
   - Stay adaptable to changing environments and technologies.

10. Use mindfulness techniques:
   - Incorporate mindfulness and meditation practices to enhance concentration and reduce the urge to engage with digital distractions.

By implementing these strategies, individuals and organizations can better manage time in the digital age, leading to increased productivity, reduced stress, and improved work-life balance.

Strategies for digital workplace wellness:

Creating a healthy digital workplace involves implementing strategies that prioritize both productivity and employee well-being. Here are some effective strategies to promote digital wellness in the workplace:

1. Leadership and Culture

- Lead by Example: Leaders should model healthy digital habits, such as setting boundaries for work-related communications outside of office hours.

- Promote a Culture of Balance: Encourage a workplace culture that values work-life balance and respects employees' time away from digital devices.

2. Digital Detox Initiatives

- Digital Sabbaticals: Encourage employees to take regular breaks from digital devices, such as tech-free weekends or designated "unplugged" hours during the workday.
- Unplug Zones: Designate specific areas in the office where technology use is discouraged, promoting face-to-face interactions and focused work.

3. Clear Digital Boundaries

- Define Work Hours: Clearly communicate expectations regarding work hours and digital communication outside those times.
- Respect the Off Switch: Avoid sending emails or messages during non-working hours to respect employees' personal time.

4. Education and Training

- Digital Wellness Workshops: Organize workshops on topics like digital minimalism, time management, and managing digital distractions.
- Provide Resources: Share articles, apps, and other resources that promote healthy tech use and mindfulness practices.

5. Use of Technology for Good

- Well-being Technologies: Implement tools that help monitor and manage work habits and stress levels, providing insights into employee wellness.
- Collaborative Tools: Use technology to enhance workplace connections, scheduling regular check-ins and virtual social events to foster a sense of community.

6. Regular Assessment and Feedback

- Conduct Assessments: Regularly evaluate the digital health of the organization through surveys and focus groups to understand employee challenges and needs.
- Tailor Well-being Plans: Develop digital well-being plans based on feedback, setting clear objectives and measurable outcomes.

7. Recognition and Incentives

- Celebrate Successes: Recognize and reward employees who actively contribute to a healthier digital environment, reinforcing positive behaviors.
- Offer Incentives: Consider offering bonuses or time off for employees who participate in digital detox challenges.

By implementing these strategies, organizations can create a digital workplace that supports both productivity and employee well-being, fostering a healthier, more balanced work environment.

Remote work and digital boundaries:

Based on the search results, here are key points about remote work and digital boundaries:

1. Flexible and permeable boundaries:
- Remote work has led to more flexible boundaries (shifting work to different times/locations) and permeable boundaries (work bleeding into personal life and vice versa).
- This blurring of work-home boundaries was accelerated by the COVID-19 pandemic.

2. Impact on job satisfaction:
- More work flexibility tends to increase job satisfaction.
- More work permeability tends to decrease job satisfaction.

3. Setting clear boundaries is important:
- Establish dedicated work hours and communicate them to colleagues.
- Create "tech-free zones" in your home where work devices are not allowed.
- Set specific times for checking emails/messages rather than being always available.

4. Managing digital communication:
- Follow the "10% rule" - decline meetings where you'll participate less than 10% of the time.
- Be intentional about your schedule and communicate it clearly to teammates.
- Set expectations around response times for emails/messages outside work hours.

5. Workspace considerations:
- Have a dedicated workspace if possible to create physical separation between work and home.
- Be clear about whether you are fully remote or expected to come into an office occasionally.

6. Company culture:
- Organizations should set clear guidelines and expectations around remote work.
- Fostering a culture that respects boundaries and work-life balance is important.

7. Self-management:
- Be proactive in communicating and enforcing your boundaries.
- Use time management techniques like the Pomodoro method.
- Practice digital mindfulness to reduce distractions.

8. Challenges:
- Remote workers may feel pressure to always be available.
- Managers may not have visibility into workloads, leading to overwork.
- Time zone differences can complicate scheduling and availability.

The key is finding a balance that allows for productivity and collaboration while also protecting personal time and preventing burnout in a remote work environment. Clear communication and intentional boundary-setting are crucial.

Chapter 7: Digital Citizenship and Safety

Digital citizenship refers to the responsible and ethical use of technology and online platforms. This chapter explores the key aspects of being a good digital citizen and staying safe in the digital world.

Understanding Digital Citizenship

Digital citizenship encompasses:

1. Responsible use of technology
2. Ethical online behavior
3. Digital literacy and critical thinking
4. Online safety and security awareness
5. Respect for others in digital spaces

Key Elements of Digital Citizenship

1. Digital Etiquette

- Practicing good manners online
- Being respectful in digital communications
- Understanding cultural differences in online interactions

2. Digital Rights and Responsibilities

- Knowing your rights in the digital world
- Understanding copyright and fair use
- Respecting others' intellectual property

3. Digital Literacy

- Ability to find, evaluate, and use online information critically
- Understanding how to use various digital tools and platforms
- Recognizing misinformation and fake news

4. Digital Security

- Protecting personal information online
- Using strong passwords and two-factor authentication
- Being aware of phishing and other online scams

5. Digital Health and Wellness

- Balancing screen time with offline activities
- Recognizing and mitigating digital addiction
- Understanding the impact of technology on mental and physical health

Promoting Online Safety

1. Privacy Protection:
   - Adjust privacy settings on social media platforms
   - Be cautious about sharing personal information online

2. Cyberbullying Prevention:
   - Recognize signs of cyberbullying
   - Know how to report and address online harassment

3. Safe Social Networking:
   - Be mindful of what you share on social media
   - Understand the potential long-term impacts of online posts

4. Secure Online Transactions:
   - Use secure websites for online shopping and banking
   - Be wary of suspicious emails or requests for financial information

5. Data Protection:
   - Regularly update software and use antivirus programs
   - Back up important data and use encryption when necessary

Teaching Digital Citizenship

1. Incorporate digital citizenship into school curricula
2. Provide resources for parents to guide children's online behavior
3. Encourage open discussions about online experiences and challenges
4. Model good digital citizenship as educators and leaders

The Future of Digital Citizenship

As technology continues to evolve, so too will the concept of digital citizenship. Emerging areas of focus include:

1. Artificial Intelligence ethics
2. Virtual and augmented reality etiquette
3. Blockchain and cryptocurrency literacy
4. Internet of Things (IoT) security awareness

By embracing and promoting digital citizenship, we can create a safer, more respectful, and more productive digital world for all users.

Online privacy and security:

Online Privacy and Security

Online privacy and security are critical components of digital citizenship, focusing on protecting personal information and ensuring safe online interactions. Here is an overview of these concepts and strategies to enhance them:

Understanding Online Privacy

Online privacy, also known as digital or internet privacy, involves the protection and control of personal information shared on the internet. It encompasses:

- Personal Data Protection: Safeguarding sensitive information such as names, addresses, financial details, and browsing habits from unauthorized access.
- Data Control: Users' ability to decide what information they share and with whom, including third-party data usage.

- Digital Footprint Management: Being aware of the trail of data left behind when using online services and platforms.

Importance of Online Privacy

1. Protection Against Cyber Attacks: Reducing the amount of personal data available online can help prevent cyber threats such as identity theft, phishing, and malware attacks.

2. Autonomy and Control: Maintaining privacy allows individuals to have control over their personal information and how it is used by companies and governments.

3. Preventing Data Exploitation: Personal data is often used for targeted advertising, profiling, and other commercial purposes, making privacy crucial for preventing exploitation.

Online Security

Online security refers to measures taken to protect against cyber threats and unauthorized access to personal data. Key components include:

- Strong Passwords: Using complex, unique passwords for different accounts.
- Two-Factor Authentication: Adding an extra layer of security by requiring a second form of verification.
- Secure Connections: Utilizing HTTPS and VPNs to encrypt data and protect privacy online.

Strategies for Enhancing Online Privacy and Security

1. Use Privacy Settings: Adjust privacy settings on social media and other online accounts to limit data sharing.

2. Be Cautious with Personal Information: Avoid sharing sensitive details publicly and be mindful of the information provided to websites and apps.

3. Regularly Update Software: Keep devices and applications updated to protect against vulnerabilities and security threats.

4. Educate Yourself: Stay informed about online privacy rights and best practices for maintaining security.

5. Use Privacy Tools: Consider using ad blockers, anti-tracking browser extensions, and secure search engines to enhance privacy.

6. Monitor Digital Footprint: Regularly review what personal information is available online and take steps to remove or secure it if necessary.

By understanding and implementing these strategies, individuals can better protect their online privacy and ensure a safer digital experience.

Digital footprint management:

Digital footprint management involves actively controlling and protecting the information you leave behind online. Here are key strategies for managing your digital footprint:

1. Understand your digital footprint:
- Conduct regular searches of your name and personal information to see what's publicly available.
- Be aware of both active (information you intentionally share) and passive (data collected about your online activities) digital footprints.

2. Protect personal information:
- Use strong, unique passwords for different accounts.
- Enable two-factor authentication where possible.
- Be cautious about sharing sensitive information online.
- Avoid using public Wi-Fi for logging into important accounts.

3. Manage privacy settings:
- Regularly review and adjust privacy settings on social media and other online accounts.
- Limit the personal information visible to non-connections on social media.

4. Be mindful of social media use:
- Think carefully before posting personal information or opinions.
- Regularly update your friend lists and use targeted sharing features.
- Consider the long-term implications of your posts.

5. Use privacy-enhancing tools:
- Utilize Virtual Private Networks (VPNs) to hide your IP address.
- Use secure and private browsers.
- Consider using ad blockers and anti-tracking extensions.

6. Manage search engine results:
- Submit removal requests for personal information appearing in search results.
- Create positive content to influence your online presence.

7. Be cautious with online activities:
- Be aware that online shopping, banking, and news subscriptions contribute to your digital footprint.
- Read privacy policies and terms of service before using new apps or services.

8. Use digital footprint management tools:
- Consider using services like Optery, Incogni, or DeleteMe to remove personal information from data broker sites.
- Utilize tools like Cover Your Tracks to check your browser's resistance to tracking.

9. Regularly clean up your online presence:
- Delete old accounts you no longer use.
- Remove unnecessary apps and revoke their permissions.

10. Stay informed:
- Keep up-to-date with privacy laws and your rights regarding personal data.
- Be aware of emerging technologies and their potential impact on digital privacy.

Remember, managing your digital footprint is an ongoing process that requires vigilance and regular attention. By implementing these strategies, you can better control your online presence and protect your personal information.

Cyberbullying and online harassment:

Cyberbullying and online harassment are significant issues in the digital age, affecting individuals of all ages, particularly young people. Here is an overview of these issues and strategies for prevention and intervention:

Understanding Cyberbullying and Online Harassment

Cyberbullying involves using digital platforms to send, post, or share negative, harmful, or mean content about someone. It can occur via social media, text messages, email, or other online forums and can have serious consequences, including emotional distress, anxiety, depression, and even suicidal thoughts.

Key Characteristics

- Anonymity: Perpetrators can often remain anonymous, making it difficult to hold them accountable.
- Pervasiveness: Unlike traditional bullying, cyberbullying can occur 24/7 and reach a wide audience quickly.
- Persistence: Digital content can be difficult to remove once it is shared, prolonging the victim's distress.

Strategies for Prevention and Intervention

1. Education and Awareness

- Digital Citizenship Programs: Educate students about responsible online behavior and the consequences of cyberbullying.
- Social Skills Training: Teach young people how to communicate effectively and resolve conflicts online.

2. Empowerment and Support

- Encourage Reporting: Create a supportive environment where victims feel safe reporting cyberbullying incidents.
- Parental Engagement: Involve parents in monitoring online activities and educating them on how to support their children.

3. Practical Measures

- Privacy Settings: Use privacy tools to control who can see personal information and posts online.

- Strong Passwords: Protect accounts with strong, unique passwords to prevent unauthorized access.

4. Response Strategies

- Do Not Respond Immediately: Advice victims to take time before responding to avoid emotional reactions.
- Take Screenshots: Document evidence of cyberbullying to report to authorities or platform administrators.
- Limit Screen Time: Reduce exposure to online harassment by taking breaks from social media and other platforms.

5. Reporting and Blocking

- Use Platform Tools: Most social media sites have built-in tools for reporting and blocking cyberbullies.
- Seek Professional Help: Encourage victims to seek counseling or support from professionals if needed.

Role of Schools and Communities

- Policy Development: Schools should have clear policies and procedures for dealing with cyberbullying incidents.
- Community Involvement: Engage community organizations in raising awareness and providing resources for prevention and support.

By implementing these strategies, individuals, schools, and communities can work together to prevent cyberbullying and support those affected by it, fostering a safer and more respectful online environment.

Legal and ethical considerations in the digital space:

Navigating the digital space involves understanding various legal and ethical considerations that impact individuals, businesses, and governments. Here are some key aspects:

Legal Considerations

1. Regulatory Frameworks:
  - The Digital Services Act (DSA) in the EU aims to create a safer and more transparent digital environment by harmonizing rules for intermediary services and addressing illegal content and disinformation.
  - The regulation of digital assets, such as cryptocurrencies, requires understanding the legal concepts behind these assets and may necessitate adjustments to existing laws.

2. Privacy and Data Protection:
  - Laws such as the General Data Protection Regulation (GDPR) in the EU set standards for data protection and privacy, requiring organizations to handle personal data responsibly.

3. Intellectual Property:
  - Protecting intellectual property rights online involves understanding copyright, trademark, and patent laws, and ensuring that digital content is used legally.

4. Content Regulation:
  - Laws like the French SREN Act focus on protecting minors from harmful content and combating online scams, hate, and misinformation.

Ethical Considerations

1. Digital Rights and Responsibilities:
  - Digital citizens have rights such as privacy and free speech, but they also have responsibilities to use technology ethically and respect others' rights.

2. Algorithmic Fairness:
  - The use of algorithms in decision-making processes raises ethical questions about bias, transparency, and accountability.

3. Cybersecurity Ethics:
  - Ethical considerations in cybersecurity include protecting user data, preventing unauthorized access, and ensuring the integrity of digital systems.

4. Digital Inclusion:
   - Ensuring equitable access to digital technologies and addressing the digital divide are important ethical considerations in promoting digital citizenship.

In summary, navigating the digital space requires a comprehensive understanding of both legal frameworks and ethical principles. By adhering to these considerations, individuals and organizations can foster a safer, more equitable, and respectful digital environment.

Chapter 8: Digital Wellness for Special Needs:

Chapter 8: Digital Wellness for Special Needs

Digital wellness for individuals with special needs is an important area that requires tailored approaches and considerations. This chapter explores how digital technologies can be both beneficial and challenging for people with disabilities and special educational needs (SEN).

Benefits of Digital Technology for Special Needs

1. Accessibility and Inclusion:
   - Digital services can be lifelines for children with disabilities, offering ways to participate, engage, learn, and play at their own pace.
   - Virtual forums and support groups provide spaces for connection and community.

2. Assistive Features:
   - Digital location imaging can help those with mobility support needs find wheelchair-accessible areas.
   - Voice, chat, translation, and video functions offer flexibility and alternatives for different needs.

3. Educational Support:
   - Adaptive learning technologies can provide personalized educational experiences.
   - Digital tools can help with organization, time management, and task completion.

Challenges and Risks

1. Increased Vulnerability:
   - Children with SEN report being bullied 12% more online than their non-disabled peers.
   - Higher susceptibility to financial exploitation, particularly on social media.

2. Exposure to Harmful Content:
   - Parents of children with SEN report seeing three times as many instances of upsetting online content compared to parents of non-SEN children.

3. Privacy Concerns:
   - Parents of children with SEN are twice as likely to worry about their child's online privacy.
   - One-third of children with physical disabilities have experienced their social media accounts being hacked.

4. Misinformation:
   - Circulation of dangerous "miracle cures" for conditions like autism can negatively impact self-esteem, health, and wellbeing.

Strategies for Promoting Digital Wellness

1. Tailored Education:
   - Develop digital citizenship programs specifically designed for individuals with special needs.
   - Provide social skills training focused on online communication and conflict resolution.

2. Adaptive Technologies:
   - Utilize assistive technologies and accessibility features to enhance the digital experience.
   - Encourage the development of apps and platforms designed with special needs in mind.

3. Supportive Communities:
   - Foster online communities that provide safe spaces for individuals with special needs to connect and share experiences.
   - Encourage peer support and mentoring programs.

4. Parental and Caregiver Involvement:
   - Educate parents and caregivers on how to support and monitor their children's online activities.
   - Provide resources for addressing specific challenges related to different disabilities.

5. Collaboration with Healthcare Providers:
   - Integrate digital wellness strategies into overall health and therapy plans.
   - Utilize telehealth services to provide ongoing support and monitoring.

By addressing both the opportunities and challenges of digital technology for individuals with special needs, we can work towards creating a more inclusive and supportive digital environment. This approach ensures that everyone, regardless of their abilities, can benefit from the digital world while minimizing potential risks.

Adapting digital tools for diverse abilities:

Adapting digital tools for diverse abilities involves leveraging technology to create inclusive and accessible learning environments for individuals with varying needs. Here are some key strategies and considerations:

Assistive Technologies

1. Text-to-Speech and Speech-to-Text Tools:
  - These tools help students with reading and writing difficulties by converting text to audio and spoken words to text, respectively. Examples include NaturalReader and speech recognition systems.

2. Alternative Input Devices:
  - Devices such as alternative keyboards, trackballs, and joysticks assist students with mobility impairments in accessing computers and digital content.

3. Screen Readers and Magnification Software:
  - Tools like screen readers convert text to speech, aiding visually impaired students in accessing digital materials. Magnification software enlarges content for easier viewing.

4. Closed Captioning and Subtitles:
  - Providing captions for audio content helps students with hearing impairments fully engage with multimedia resources.

Adaptive Learning Platforms

- Digital platforms can offer personalized learning experiences by adapting content and assessments to the individual needs of each student. This approach helps in catering to diverse learning styles and paces.

Inclusive Design Principles

1. Universal Design for Learning (UDL):

- UDL principles advocate for designing educational materials and activities that are accessible to all learners, regardless of their abilities or disabilities.

2. Accessibility Features:
  - Developers should incorporate accessibility features into digital tools and platforms, ensuring they are usable by everyone. This includes customizable text sizes, color contrasts, and navigation options.

Overcoming Challenges

1. Digital Divide:
  - Addressing the digital divide is crucial to ensure all students have equal access to technology and digital resources, regardless of their socio-economic status.

2. Professional Development:
  - Continuous training for educators is essential to effectively integrate digital tools into teaching practices and to support students with diverse needs.

3. Ongoing Evaluation:
  - Regular assessment of the impact of digital tools on learning outcomes helps in refining and improving their use in educational settings.

By thoughtfully integrating digital tools and assistive technologies, educators can create more inclusive learning environments that empower all students to reach their full potential.

Assistive technologies and digital inclusion:

Assistive Technologies and Digital Inclusion

Assistive technologies and digital inclusion are crucial for ensuring that individuals with disabilities can fully participate in educational, professional, and social activities. These technologies and approaches aim to remove barriers and create a more inclusive digital environment.

Understanding Assistive Technologies

Assistive technology refers to devices, software, or equipment designed to enhance the capabilities and independence of individuals with disabilities. These technologies help individuals perform tasks that might otherwise be challenging or impossible. Examples include:

- Screen Readers: Convert text into speech or braille, aiding visually impaired individuals in accessing digital content.
- Alternative Input Devices: Such as joysticks or voice recognition software, which assist people with mobility impairments in operating computers.
- Speech-to-Text Applications: Convert spoken words into written text, supporting individuals with dyslexia or writing difficulties.
- Adaptive Keyboards: Customized keyboards that cater to specific motor skills or accessibility needs.

Digital Inclusion

Digital inclusion focuses on ensuring that everyone, regardless of their abilities, can access and benefit from digital technologies. It involves:

- Accessibility: Designing digital content and technologies to be usable by people with disabilities. This includes providing alternative text for images, ensuring keyboard navigation support, and implementing captioning for multimedia content.
- Equal Opportunities: Ensuring that digital platforms offer equal opportunities to all individuals, eliminating discrimination based on disability.

Broader User Base: Embracing digital accessibility benefits not only individuals with disabilities but also older adults, people with temporary impairments, or those using mobile devices.

Benefits of Assistive Technology and Digital Inclusion

1. Independence and Inclusion: Assistive technology empowers individuals with disabilities to participate fully in various activities, promoting independence.
2. Enhanced Productivity: These technologies improve efficiency and productivity by enabling individuals to overcome challenges and perform tasks more effectively.

3. Compliance and Legal Requirements: Many countries have laws enforcing digital accessibility, ensuring organizations avoid legal issues and demonstrate commitment to inclusivity.

Challenges and Considerations

1. Design and Usability: Poor design and difficult content can negatively affect user experiences. It's crucial to develop user-centered digital content and products.
2. Digital Divide: Not all individuals have equal access to technology, which can exacerbate inequalities. Efforts must be made to bridge this gap.
3. Ongoing Professional Development: Continuous training for educators and developers is essential to integrate assistive technologies effectively.

Future of Assistive Technology and Digital Inclusion

The future holds immense promise for inclusion with advancements in artificial intelligence, machine learning, and natural language processing. These technologies offer new opportunities for creating more robust and user-friendly assistive tools, such as smart home devices and wearable technologies.

By embracing assistive technologies and digital inclusion, we can create a more equitable and accessible digital world, ensuring that no one is left behind.

Strategies for caregivers and educators:

Based on the search results and the context of digital wellness for special needs, here are some strategies for caregivers and educators working with individuals with special needs in the digital space:

1. Personalize digital learning experiences:
   - Adapt digital tools and content to suit individual needs and abilities.
   - Use assistive technologies like screen readers, speech-to-text tools, or alternative input devices as needed.

2. Prioritize digital safety and privacy:
   - Educate individuals with special needs about online safety, privacy, and potential risks.
   - Implement appropriate parental controls or monitoring tools when necessary.

3. Foster digital inclusion:
   - Ensure that digital activities and platforms are accessible to all, regardless of abilities.
   - Promote inclusive design principles in digital tools and content creation.

4. Provide structured digital routines:
   - Establish clear schedules for device use and online activities.
   - Use visual schedules or reminders to help individuals manage their digital time.

5. Encourage balanced technology use:
   - Promote a healthy mix of online and offline activities.
   - Teach self-regulation skills for managing screen time.

6. Leverage technology for communication:
   - Use digital tools to enhance communication skills, especially for non-verbal individuals.
   - Explore augmentative and alternative communication (AAC) devices or apps.

7. Collaborate with support networks:
   - Work closely with families, therapists, and other educators to ensure consistent approaches to digital use.
   - Share resources and strategies across the support network.

8. Stay informed about assistive technologies:
   - Keep up-to-date with the latest assistive technologies and digital tools designed for special needs.
   - Attend workshops or training sessions on using these technologies effectively.

9. Practice digital empathy:
   - Be patient and understanding when individuals struggle with digital tasks.
   - Celebrate small victories in digital skill development.

10. Monitor and adjust strategies:
   - Regularly assess the effectiveness of digital tools and approaches.
   - Be flexible and willing to adjust strategies based on individual progress and changing needs.

11. Promote digital independence:
   - Gradually increase autonomy in digital activities as skills improve.
   - Teach problem-solving skills for common digital issues.

12. Address sensory needs:
   - Be mindful of sensory sensitivities when using digital devices (e.g., screen brightness, volume levels).
   - Provide sensory breaks during extended periods of digital engagement.

By implementing these strategies, caregivers and educators can help individuals with special needs navigate the digital world more effectively, ensuring they benefit from technology while minimizing potential challenges.

Chapter 9: Environmental Impact of Digital Habits:

The environmental impact of our digital habits is a growing concern as technology becomes increasingly integrated into our daily lives. This chapter explores the ecological footprint of digital technologies and provides strategies for more sustainable digital practices.

Understanding Digital Pollution

Digital pollution refers to the environmental impact caused by the production, use, and disposal of digital devices and infrastructure. Key points include:

1. Greenhouse Gas Emissions:
   - Digital technology is responsible for approximately 4% of global greenhouse gas emissions.
   - This figure could double to 8% by 2025 according to some estimates.

2. Energy Consumption:
   - By 2030, digital technologies could consume up to 51% of global electricity.
   - Data centers, networks, and user devices all contribute to this energy demand.

3. E-Waste:
   - The rapid turnover of digital devices contributes significantly to electronic waste.
   - Proper recycling and disposal of e-waste remain major challenges.

Sources of Digital Environmental Impact

1. Device Manufacturing:
   - Production of smartphones, computers, and other devices requires extensive resources and energy.
   - Mining for rare earth elements and other materials has significant environmental consequences.

2. Network Infrastructure:
   - Undersea cables, cell towers, and other network components have physical impacts on ecosystems2.

3. Data Centers:
   - The energy-intensive nature of data centers contributes substantially to the carbon footprint of digital services.

4. User Behavior:
   - Streaming videos, cloud storage, and even simple actions like sending emails all have cumulative environmental impacts.

Strategies for Eco-Friendly Digital Habits

1. Digital Sobriety:
   - Practice mindful use of digital devices and services.
   - Limit unnecessary screen time and data consumption.

2. Extend Device Lifespan:
   - Use devices for longer periods before upgrading.
   - Repair and refurbish when possible.

3. Energy Efficiency:
   - Choose energy-efficient devices and settings.
   - Optimize power management on all devices.

4. Sustainable Streaming:
   - Reduce video streaming quality when high resolution isn't necessary.
   - Download content for offline viewing instead of repeated streaming4.

5. Cloud Storage Management:
   - Regularly clean up cloud storage to reduce data center load.
   - Use local storage for less frequently accessed files.

6. Eco-Friendly Search Habits:
   - Use search engines that invest in carbon offset programs.
   - Bookmark frequently visited sites to reduce repeated searches.

Industry Responsibility and Innovation

1. Renewable Energy:

- Support companies transitioning to renewable energy sources for their digital infrastructure.

2. Circular Economy:
  - Encourage manufacturers to design for longevity, repairability, and recyclability.

3. Green Data Centers:
  - Promote the development and use of energy-efficient data center technologies.

4. Transparency:
  - Advocate for clear reporting of the environmental impact of digital services and products.

While digital technologies offer numerous benefits, it's crucial to recognize and mitigate their environmental impact. By adopting more sustainable digital habits and supporting eco-friendly innovations in the tech industry, we can help reduce the ecological footprint of our digital lives. As individuals and societies, we must strive for a balance between technological progress and environmental stewardship.

The carbon footprint of our digital lives:

The carbon footprint of our digital lives is a growing concern as technology becomes increasingly integrated into our daily activities. Here are some key points about the environmental impact of our digital habits:

1. Scale of the impact:
  - Digital technologies account for approximately 4% of global greenhouse gas emissions1.
  - If digital technology were a country, it would have an ecological output 2-3 times the size of France.

2. Sources of digital carbon footprint:
  - Hardware manufacturing and disposal (e.g. smartphones, computers, servers)
  - Energy consumption of devices during use.
  - Network infrastructure (e.g. data centers, undersea cables)
  - Data transfer and storage.

3. Specific digital activities and their impact:
   - Streaming video and music
   - Cloud storage and computing
   - Social media usage
   - Email and messaging
   - Online gaming

4. Factors influencing individual digital carbon footprints:
   - Number of devices owned and frequency of upgrades
   - Duration and type of online activities
   - Location (due to differences in energy sources).

5. Misconceptions:
   - The impact of individual digital activities is often overestimated. For example, claims about gaming having a carbon footprint comparable to flights are likely exaggerated.

6. Positive aspects:
   - The ICT sector's carbon footprint has remained relatively stable at around 1.4% of global emissions despite increased usage.
   - Digital technologies can contribute to fighting climate change through data analysis, prediction of weather events, and improving energy efficiency.

7. Potential for improvement:
   - The ICT sector's carbon footprint could be reduced by over 80% if all electricity consumed came from renewable energy sources.
   - Ongoing improvements in energy efficiency of data transmission and storage.

8. Cryptocurrency considerations:
   - Cryptocurrencies, particularly Bitcoin, have a significant carbon footprint. A single Bitcoin transaction is associated with approximately 402 kg of carbon dioxide emissions3.

Understanding the environmental impact of our digital lives is crucial for making informed decisions about our technology use and supporting sustainable digital practices.

E-waste and responsible tech disposal:

The management and disposal of electronic waste (e-waste) are critical issues due to the environmental and health risks posed by discarded electronic devices. Here are key strategies and considerations for responsible tech disposal:

Understanding E-Waste

E-waste includes discarded electronic and electrical devices such as smartphones, computers, televisions, and large appliances. These items often contain hazardous substances like lead, mercury, and cadmium, which can contaminate soil and water if not disposed of properly.

Challenges in E-Waste Management

1. Volume and Growth: The rapid expansion of technology leads to increasing amounts of e-waste, with millions of tons generated globally each year.
2. Hazardous Materials: E-waste contains toxic materials that pose environmental and health risks if improperly handled.
3. Inadequate Infrastructure: Many regions lack the necessary infrastructure for efficient e-waste collection and recycling.

Strategies for Responsible E-Waste Disposal

1. Enhance Recycling Infrastructure:
  - Develop and expand e-waste recycling facilities to handle increasing volumes efficiently.
  - Implement advanced sorting and recycling technologies to maximize material recovery.

2. Promote Circular Economy:
  - Encourage the reuse and refurbishment of electronic devices to extend their lifespan and reduce waste.
  - Adopt circular economy models that focus on recycling and reusing materials to minimize the demand for new resources.

3. Implement Strict Regulations:
  - Establish and enforce laws and regulations for e-waste management, including mandatory recycling and disposal guidelines.

- Provide incentives for consumers and businesses to participate in e-waste recycling programs.

4. Educate and Raise Awareness:
   - Increase public awareness about the environmental impact of e-waste and the importance of responsible disposal.
   - Educate consumers on how to properly dispose of electronic devices and the benefits of recycling.

5. Encourage Manufacturer Responsibility:
   - Implement Extended Producer Responsibility (EPR) policies, requiring manufacturers to take back and recycle their products at the end of their lifecycle.
   - Encourage eco-design practices that make products easier to repair, upgrade, and recycle.

6. Support Informal Sector Integration:
   - Provide training and resources to integrate informal e-waste collectors into formal recycling processes, ensuring safe and environmentally sound practices.

7. Innovative Recycling Techniques:
   - Utilize advanced recycling methods such as hydrometallurgy and pyrometallurgy to efficiently recover valuable materials from e-waste.

By adopting these strategies, we can mitigate the environmental impact of e-waste, conserve natural resources, and protect human health, contributing to a more sustainable future.

Sustainable digital practices:

Based on the search results, here are some key sustainable digital practices:

1. Optimize data management:
- Implement sound data retention policies to avoid unnecessary storage
- Use tools like the Data Carbon Ladder to determine appropriate data set sizes and storage locations
- Practice good information governance to reduce indiscriminate data retention

2. Reduce energy consumption:
- Cut back on electric waste from IT operations
- Optimize server and data center efficiency
- Use energy-efficient hardware and equipment

3. Adopt sustainable software development practices:
- Design efficient algorithms and code to minimize processing requirements
- Implement "green coding" principles to reduce energy usage

4. Optimize digital communications:
- Reduce unnecessary video conferencing or lower video quality when possible
- Be mindful of email usage and attachments

5. Extend device lifecycles:
- Use devices for longer before upgrading
- Repair and refurbish equipment when possible
- Responsibly recycle e-waste

6. Choose sustainable suppliers:
- Select cloud and hosting providers with strong environmental commitments
- Consider sustainability in IT procurement decisions

7. Raise awareness:
- Educate employees on sustainable digital habits
- Promote a culture of digital sustainability in the workplace

8. Measure and monitor:
- Track IT-related energy usage and emissions
- Set targets for improvement and regularly assess progress

9. Design for accessibility and inclusion:
- Ensure digital products and services are accessible to all users
- Bridge the digital divide by supporting digital literacy initiatives

10. Consider ethical AI development:
- Develop AI systems aligned with principles of fairness and transparency
- Assess the environmental impact of AI/ML model training and deployment

By implementing these practices, organizations can significantly reduce the environmental impact of their digital operations while often also improving efficiency and cost-effectiveness. The key is to take a holistic approach that considers sustainability throughout the digital lifecycle.

Chapter 10: Digital Literacy and Education:

Digital literacy has become an essential skill in today's technology-driven world. This chapter explores the importance of digital literacy in education and strategies for developing these skills.

Understanding Digital Literacy

Digital literacy encompasses the ability to use digital technologies effectively, critically evaluate digital information, and participate responsibly in digital environments. Key components include:

1. Technical skills to operate digital devices and software
2. Information literacy to find, evaluate, and use online information
3. Media literacy to understand and create digital media
4. Communication and collaboration skills in digital spaces
5. Digital citizenship and online safety awareness

The Importance of Digital Literacy in Education

1. Prepares students for the modern workforce
2. Enhances learning experiences through technology integration
3. Develops critical thinking and problem-solving skills
4. Promotes lifelong learning in a rapidly changing digital landscape
5. Bridges the digital divide and promotes equity in education

Strategies for Developing Digital Literacy in Education

1. Integrate technology across the curriculum:
   - Use digital tools and resources in various subjects
   - Encourage students to create digital content as part of assignments

2. Teach information literacy skills:
   - Guide students in evaluating online sources for credibility and bias
   - Develop research skills using digital resources

3. Promote digital citizenship:
   - Teach responsible and ethical use of technology
   - Address online safety, privacy, and cyberbullying

4. Provide hands-on experiences:
   - Offer opportunities to work with various digital tools and platforms
   - Encourage experimentation and problem-solving with technology

5. Professional development for educators:
   - Train teachers in digital literacy skills and technology integration
   - Keep educators updated on emerging technologies and best practices

6. Collaborate with libraries and media centers:
   - Leverage resources and expertise of school librarians
   - Create digital literacy programs and workshops

7. Assess digital literacy skills:
   - Develop assessment tools to measure students' digital competencies
   - Use results to inform curriculum development and instruction

Challenges and Considerations

1. Addressing the digital divide:
   - Ensure equitable access to technology and internet connectivity
   - Provide support for students with limited technology access at home

2. Keeping pace with technological changes:
   - Regularly update curriculum and resources to reflect new technologies
   - Foster adaptability and lifelong learning skills

3. Balancing screen time and traditional learning methods:
   - Integrate technology thoughtfully without overreliance
   - Maintain a balance between digital and non-digital learning experiences

4. Addressing concerns about data privacy and security:
   - Teach students about online privacy and data protection
   - Implement robust data security measures in educational institutions

By prioritizing digital literacy in education, we can empower students to navigate the digital world confidently, critically, and responsibly, preparing them for success in their personal and professional lives.

Improving digital literacy skills:

Improving digital literacy skills is essential for navigating the modern digital landscape effectively. Here are some strategies and insights drawn from the search results:

Key Strategies for Improving Digital Literacy

1. Education and Training:
  - Enroll in digital training programs and courses to stay updated with emerging technologies and enhance digital skills.
  - Schools and educational institutions should integrate digital literacy into their curriculums, providing access to digital resources and tools.

2. Practical Application:
  - Encourage hands-on experience with digital tools to build confidence and competence.
  - Use digital tools for organizing and managing tasks, such as online calendars and to-do lists.

3. Critical Thinking and Evaluation:
  - Develop the ability to critically evaluate digital content, discern between reliable and unreliable sources, and recognize misinformation.
  - Cultivate a questioning mindset and practice fact-checking to combat misinformation.

4. Collaboration and Communication:
  - Foster collaboration and communication skills using digital platforms, such as discussion boards and collaborative writing tools.
  - Engage in online communities to share knowledge and learn from others.

5. Digital Citizenship and Safety:
  - Teach responsible and ethical use of technology, focusing on online safety and privacy.
  - Educate individuals about digital rights and responsibilities to promote safe online behavior.

6. Lifelong Learning:
   - Embrace a mindset of continuous learning to adapt to the dynamic digital landscape.
   - Stay informed about the latest digital trends and best practices through online courses, webinars, and tutorials.

7. Bridging the Digital Divide:
   - Ensure equitable access to technology and training, particularly for vulnerable and excluded populations.
   - Address barriers to accessing digital tools and resources to promote inclusivity.

By implementing these strategies, individuals can enhance their digital literacy skills, enabling them to navigate the digital world with confidence and responsibility. This not only benefits personal and professional growth but also contributes to building a more informed and resilient society.

Digital wellness in schools and universities:

Digital wellness in schools and universities is an essential aspect of modern education, focusing on promoting healthy technology use among students and staff. Here are some strategies and insights from the search results:

Strategies for Promoting Digital Wellness

1. Open Conversations and Education:
   - Encourage transparent discussions with students about the impact of technology on their well-being, including topics like screen time, blue light exposure, and online behavior.
   - Use digital citizenship lessons to teach students about privacy protection, evaluating online sources, and managing their digital footprint.

2. Parental and Community Engagement:
   - Involve parents by providing workshops and resources on managing screen time and understanding digital risks.
   - Encourage parents to participate in initiatives like "device-free dinners" to promote offline interactions.

3. Holistic and Coordinated Approaches:
   - Implement a unified strategy across educational institutions to address digital wellness, involving stakeholders from different campuses and departments.
   - Develop policies and practices that integrate digital wellness into the broader educational framework.

4. Practical Activities and Challenges:
   - Organize classroom activities that challenge students to reduce screen time or refrain from using certain apps, encouraging self-reflection and discussion.
   - Use apps and tools to track and manage device usage, promoting awareness of digital habits.

5. Professional Development for Educators:
   - Provide training for teachers to enhance their digital literacy and equip them with the skills to support students' digital well-being.
   - Encourage continuous learning and adaptation to new digital tools and trends.

6. Digital Safety and Security:
   - Educate students and staff on online safety, data privacy, and the ethical use of digital resources.
   - Use content filtering and monitoring technologies to protect students from harmful online content.

Benefits of Digital Wellness Initiatives

- Enhanced Student Well-being: By promoting balanced technology use, students can improve their mental and physical health, reducing stress and anxiety associated with excessive screen time.
- Improved Academic Performance: Encouraging mindful technology use can help students focus better and engage more effectively in their studies.
- Empowered Digital Citizens: Teaching digital literacy and citizenship prepares students to navigate the digital world responsibly and confidently.

By integrating digital wellness into educational practices, schools and universities can create a supportive environment that fosters healthy technology use and prepares students for the challenges of the digital age.

Resources for educators and parents:

Here are some valuable resources for educators and parents aimed at improving digital literacy and promoting responsible technology use:

Digital Literacy Resources

1. Common Sense Education:
  - A nonprofit organization providing a wealth of resources for teaching digital literacy, including lesson plans, videos, and activities focused on integrating technology into the classroom.
  - Website: Common Sense Education (https://www.commonsense.org/education/)

2. DigitalLearn.org:
  - A comprehensive platform offering self-guided courses on computer basics, software applications, and job search skills. It is available in both English and Spanish, making it accessible to a wider audience.
  - Website: DigitalLearn.org (https://www.digitallearn.org)

3. GCFLearnFree.org:
  - Offers free resources covering essential skills for the 21st century, including over 2,000 lessons on topics like Microsoft Office and internet safety. Available in multiple languages.
  - Website: GCFLearnFree.org (https://www.gcflearnfree.org)

4. Mozilla Foundation:
  - Provides open-source tools and resources for educators to teach web literacy, coding, and data protection. This includes materials for facilitating community engagement.
  - Website: Mozilla Foundation (https://foundation.mozilla.org)

5. Google for Education - Applied Digital Skills:
  - A curriculum designed for educators that covers a wide range of topics. It allows integration into existing Google Classrooms or can be taught independently.
  - Website: Google for Education (https://edu.google.com/applied-digital-skills/)

Interactive Learning Platforms

6. Digital Matters:
   - A free online platform that offers interactive lessons on digital literacy and online safety for children. It includes quizzes and storytelling to engage learners effectively.
   - Website: Digital Matters (https://www.internetmatters.org/schools-esafety/digital-matters-online-learning-platform/)

7. Carnegie Cyber Academy:
   - An interactive online tool for teaching online safety practices through engaging missions and activities designed to make learning fun.
   - Website: Carnegie Cyber Academy (https://www.carnegiecyberacademy.org)

8. Media Smarts:
   - A Canadian resource that provides a framework for teaching digital literacy, including lessons on media literacy and online safety.
   - Website: Media Smarts (https://mediasmarts.ca)

Professional Development for Educators

9. Digital Learning for the K-8 Classroom:
   - An online training program designed for K-8 teachers to enhance their digital literacy skills and teaching practices.
   - Website: Teach Away (https://www.teachaway.com/blog/top-digital-literacy-resources-teachers-free-lesson-plan)

10. Microsoft Digital Literacy Curriculum:
   - Offers free online courses aimed at equipping both teachers and students with essential digital skills, including safe internet practices.
   - Website: Microsoft Digital Literacy (https://www.microsoft.com/en-us/digitalliteracy)

These resources provide a diverse array of tools and materials for educators and parents to enhance digital literacy among students and children. By utilizing these platforms, they can foster a more informed and responsible approach to technology use, preparing learners for the challenges of the digital age.

Lifelong learning in the digital age:

Lifelong learning in the digital age has become increasingly important as technology continues to evolve rapidly and reshape various aspects of our lives. Here are some key points about lifelong learning in the digital era:

1. Continuous skill development:
   - The digital age requires constant updating of skills to remain relevant in the workforce.
   - Lifelong learning helps individuals adapt to new technologies and changing job requirements.

2. Accessibility of learning resources:
   - Digital platforms provide unprecedented access to educational content and courses.
   - MOOCs, online tutorials, and digital libraries offer flexible learning opportunities.

3. Personalized learning experiences:
   - Technology enables tailored learning paths based on individual needs and preferences.
   - Adaptive learning systems can adjust content difficulty and pacing to suit each learner.

4. Informal and self-directed learning:
   - The digital age facilitates informal learning through online communities, forums, and social media.
   - Individuals can take charge of their own learning journey, exploring topics of personal interest.

5. Digital literacy as a core competency:
   - Developing digital literacy skills is crucial for effective participation in the digital society.
   - This includes the ability to critically evaluate online information and use digital tools effectively.

6. Workplace learning integration:
   - Digital technologies enable seamless integration of learning into work environments.
   - Just-in-time learning and microlearning approaches support continuous professional development.

7. Global connectivity and collaboration:
   - Digital platforms facilitate learning from diverse global perspectives.
   - Collaborative online spaces enable knowledge sharing across geographical boundaries.

8. Challenges and considerations:
   - Addressing the digital divide to ensure equitable access to learning opportunities.
   - Balancing online and offline learning experiences for holistic development.
   - Ensuring the quality and credibility of online learning resources.

9. Mindset shift:
   - Fostering a growth mindset and curiosity for continuous learning throughout life.
   - Recognizing learning as an ongoing process rather than a finite achievement.

10. Impact on well-being and social engagement:
   - Lifelong learning in the digital age can enhance mental health, resilience, and
creativity.
   - It also promotes social and civic engagement in an increasingly interconnected world.

By embracing lifelong learning in the digital age, individuals can adapt to technological
changes, enhance their personal and professional development, and contribute to a more
informed and engaged society.

Chapter 11: AI Platforms: Allies in Digital Wellness:

As artificial intelligence (AI) continues to evolve, it's increasingly being leveraged to support digital wellness initiatives. This chapter explores how AI platforms are becoming valuable allies in promoting healthier digital habits and overall well-being.

AI-Driven Wellness Tools

1. Personalized Health Coaching:
   - AI platforms like GoE Wellness offer personalized wellness programs that integrate fitness, nutrition, beauty, and mindfulness.
   - These platforms use AI to analyze user data and provide tailored recommendations for improving overall health.

2. Mental Health Support:
   - AI-powered chatbots and virtual assistants provide 24/7 access to mental health resources.
   - These tools offer real-time, empathetic conversations and can help identify early signs of stress or anxiety.

3. Stress Management:
   - AI algorithms can analyze workplace data to identify stress patterns and suggest interventions.
   - This proactive approach helps managers address potential burnout before it becomes severe.

AI in the Workplace

1. Task Automation:
   - AI tools automate repetitive tasks, reducing employee stress and allowing focus on more meaningful work.
   - Platforms like UiPath use AI to streamline data management and scheduling.

2. Employee Wellness Programs:
   - AI-driven platforms like Terryberry's walking challenge use data analysis to suggest personalized wellness activities.

- These programs promote physical activity and overall well-being in the workplace.

3. Performance Monitoring:
  - While AI monitoring tools can improve efficiency, it's crucial to balance this with employee privacy concerns.
  - Transparent communication about AI use in the workplace is essential to maintain trust and morale.

Innovative AI Applications

1. Virtual Reality for Wellness:
  - Companies like GoE Wellness are exploring VR applications for mental health and relaxation.
  - These immersive experiences can provide virtual retreats and guided meditation sessions.

2. AI-Powered Digital Detox:
  - Generative AI has the potential to create personalized "digital detox" plans.
  - These plans can suggest offline activities and help users manage their screen time more effectively.

3. Continuous Health Monitoring:
  - AI platforms like Sensights App offer continuous health monitoring for holistic well-being.
  - These tools can track various health metrics and provide insights for improving overall health.

Challenges and Considerations

1. Data Privacy and Security:
  - As AI platforms collect sensitive health data, ensuring robust data protection measures is crucial.

2. Ethical Use of AI:
  - It's important to address potential biases in AI algorithms and ensure fair and equitable wellness recommendations.

3. Balancing Technology and Human Touch:

  - While AI can provide valuable support, it's essential to maintain human connections in wellness initiatives.

4. Digital Divide:
  - Ensuring equal access to AI-powered wellness tools across different socioeconomic groups remains a challenge.

By leveraging AI platforms responsibly and ethically, organizations and individuals can harness the power of technology to promote digital wellness and overall health. As these tools continue to evolve, they have the potential to revolutionize our approach to well-being in the digital age.

Understanding AI and its role in daily life

Key points about AI and its everyday impact:

1. Definition and core concepts:
- AI refers to computer systems that can perform tasks typically requiring human intelligence
- Key components include machine learning, natural language processing, computer vision, and robotics

2. Widespread integration:
- AI is now embedded in many common devices and services we use daily
- Examples include smartphones, smart home devices, streaming services, social media, and more

3. Personal assistance:
- AI powers virtual assistants like Siri, Alexa, and Google Assistant
- These can help with tasks like scheduling, reminders, information lookup, and device control

4. Personalization and recommendations:
- AI analyzes user data to provide personalized content, product recommendations, etc.
- Used by streaming services, e-commerce sites, social media platforms

5. Automation of routine tasks:
- AI can handle repetitive tasks in areas like email filtering, data entry, customer service.

- Frees up human time and resources for more complex work

6. Enhanced decision making:
- AI can process vast amounts of data to provide insights and predictions
- Used in areas like financial services, healthcare diagnostics, weather forecasting.

7. Improved safety and security:
- AI powers things like facial recognition, fraud detection systems, and autonomous vehicle safety features.

8. Accessibility features:
- AI enables tools like real-time captioning, text-to-speech, and language translation.

9. Challenges and considerations:
- Privacy concerns around data collection and use
- Potential for bias in AI systems
- Impact on jobs and workforce

10. Ongoing evolution:
- AI capabilities are rapidly advancing
- Likely to become even more integrated into daily life in coming years

The key takeaway is that AI has become deeply woven into the fabric of modern life, often in ways that are not immediately obvious. It's enhancing convenience, productivity, and capabilities across many domains, while also raising important societal questions that need to be addressed as the technology continues to evolve.

Beneficial AI platforms for productivity:

Here are some beneficial AI platforms that can boost productivity:

1. Task Management and Project Planning:
- Motion: AI-powered task management and scheduling tool that optimizes your calendar and to-do list.
- Notion AI: Enhances Notion's organizational capabilities with AI for generating content, answering questions, and more.

2. Writing and Content Creation:
- Jasper: AI writing assistant for generating marketing copy, blog posts, social media content, etc.
- Grammarly: AI-powered writing assistant for grammar, style, and tone improvements.

3. Meeting Assistance and Transcription:
- Otter.ai: Provides real-time transcription and meeting notes with AI-powered summaries.
- Fireflies.ai: AI meeting assistant that records, transcribes, and analyzes conversations.

4. Research and Information Synthesis:
- Elicit: AI research assistant that helps find and summarize relevant academic papers.
- Perplexity AI: Combines AI with web search to provide detailed answers to complex queries.

5. Image and Design:
- DALL-E: AI image generation tool for creating unique visuals from text descriptions.
- Canva AI: Integrates AI capabilities into Canva's design platform for faster content creation.

6. Email Management:
- SaneBox: Uses AI to prioritize and organize your email inbox.
- Superhuman: AI-powered email client for faster email processing and management.

7. Presentation Creation:
- Beautiful.ai: AI-powered presentation software that automates design and layout.
- Gamma: Creates AI-generated presentations from text prompts or outlines.

8. Personal Assistance:
- ChatGPT: Versatile AI chatbot that can assist with various tasks, from writing to problem-solving.
- Claude: Another powerful AI assistant for various productivity tasks.

These AI platforms can significantly enhance productivity by automating routine tasks, providing creative assistance, and streamlining workflows across various domains. The key is to identify which tools align best with your specific needs and integrate them effectively into your work processes.

AI for health and wellness:

AI is increasingly playing a significant role in health and wellness, offering innovative solutions to enhance personal and public health management. Here are some ways AI platforms are contributing to health and wellness:

1. Mental Health Support:
   - AI-powered chatbots and platforms provide mental health support by offering real-time, empathetic conversations and resources. These tools can help reduce stress by automating repetitive tasks and analyzing workplace stress patterns to implement targeted interventions.

2. Health Monitoring and Detection:
   - AI health monitoring apps track key health indicators like steps, heart rate, and calories burned, encouraging healthier lifestyles. These apps provide personalized health advice and can predict potential health issues, such as heart problems, before they become serious.

3. Personalized Wellness Programs:
   - Platforms like AI Wellness offer personalized wellness solutions powered by AI, bridging the gap between healthcare and wellness through precision education and innovation. These tools provide continuous health monitoring and tailored care.

4. Regulatory Considerations:
   - While AI wellness apps offer significant benefits, they operate in a regulatory gray area, especially when crossing into medical territory. There are concerns about the potential health risks of these apps, particularly when they are used during mental health crises without proper oversight.

5. AI in Healthcare Mobile Apps:
   - AI is being integrated into healthcare mobile apps to improve service delivery and health outcomes. These apps, such as Noom and Ada AI Doctor, offer features like symptom tracking, health advice, and personalized health management plans.

AI platforms in health and wellness are revolutionizing how individuals manage their health, offering personalized, accessible, and efficient solutions. However, it is crucial to address regulatory challenges and ensure these technologies are used safely and effectively.

Addressing AI concerns and misconceptions:

Based on the search results, here are some key points for addressing common AI concerns and misconceptions:

1. AI bias and neutrality:
- Myth: AI models can be entirely free from bias.
- Reality: Bias inevitably exists in AI models as they learn from human-generated data. The goal is to align models with intended values and continuously monitor performance, not eliminate bias entirely.

2. AI replacing human jobs:
- Myth: AI will completely replace human roles.
- Reality: AI excels at specific tasks within roles but is unlikely to replace entire jobs. It's more likely to complement human expertise and work collaboratively on defined tasks.

3. AI capabilities and limitations:
- Myth: AI systems are conscious or sentient.
- Reality: Despite impressive capabilities, AI lacks true consciousness, emotions, or experiences. It mimics patterns but falls short of human-like sentience.

4. AI accuracy and reliability:
- Myth: AI always provides completely accurate and factual responses.
- Reality: AI models, especially large language models, can produce inaccuracies or "hallucinations." Techniques like using trusted data sources and Retrieval Augmented Generation (RAG) can improve accuracy.

5. Accessibility and implementation:
- Myth: AI is too expensive and complex for most organizations to implement.
- Reality: Transfer learning and pre-trained models make AI more accessible. Organizations can leverage existing models and customize them for specific needs.

6. AI control and predictability:
- Myth: AI systems are unpredictable and uncontrollable.

- Reality: Effective error-handling and control techniques, similar to those used in aviation and manufacturing, can be applied to manage complex AI systems.

7. Data readiness for AI:
- Myth: Organizations need perfect data before implementing AI.
- Reality: Data readiness is use-case dependent. A pragmatic approach to data preparation is more important than striving for perfection.

8. Human involvement in AI:
- Myth: AI solutions can be delivered without human involvement.
- Reality: Human expertise remains crucial for defining objectives, interpreting results, and ensuring alignment with organizational goals.

To address these concerns and misconceptions:
- Educate people about AI's actual capabilities and limitations
- Promote responsible AI development and use
- Encourage critical thinking when interacting with AI systems
- Emphasize the collaborative potential between humans and AI
- Support ongoing research and development to improve AI technologies

By addressing these misconceptions, we can foster a more informed and balanced understanding of AI's role in society and its potential impact on various aspects of our lives.

The future of AI in digital wellness:

The future of AI in digital wellness is poised to revolutionize how individuals manage their health and well-being. Here are some key insights and developments based on the search results:

1. AI Health Coaches:
   - AI-powered health coaches will offer personalized guidance by analyzing real-time data from wearable devices and biometric sensors. These coaches can provide tailored advice on sleep, stress, and physical activity, optimizing individual health outcomes.

2. Virtual Reality Wellness Experiences:
   - The integration of AI with virtual reality (VR) will create immersive wellness experiences. These VR environments can adjust dynamically based on biometric feedback, offering personalized meditation, relaxation, and fitness sessions.

3. Genetic-Based Wellness Plans:
   - AI will leverage genetic data to create personalized wellness plans. By analyzing genetic predispositions, AI can craft bespoke lifestyle modifications, nutrition plans, and exercise routines to enhance health outcomes.

4. Emotionally Intelligent Chatbots:
   - Future AI chatbots will incorporate emotional intelligence to provide empathetic support and guidance, offering personalized encouragement and mental health resources.

5. AI-Enhanced Nutritional Supplements:
   - AI will enable the development of customized nutritional supplements by analyzing dietary habits, nutrient deficiencies, and genetic markers, optimizing individual health and performance.

6. Predictive Health Monitoring:
   - AI-powered predictive analytics will allow for proactive health monitoring, identifying potential health issues early and enabling timely interventions.

7. AI-Powered Community Support Platforms:
   - AI-driven platforms will facilitate community support, enabling individuals to connect, share experiences, and access resources to achieve their wellness goals collectively.

8. Regulatory and Ethical Considerations:
   - There are concerns about the regulatory oversight of AI-based wellness apps, particularly when they cross into medical territory. Ensuring these apps do not increase the risk of harm is a challenge that needs addressing.

9. AI in Chronic Disease Management:
   - AI-powered wearables and apps offer real-time health monitoring and personalized recommendations, especially beneficial for managing chronic conditions like diabetes and heart disease.

10. Organizational Wellness:
   - AI can enhance workplace wellness through personalized wellness programs, mental health support, and promoting a healthier work-life balance.

The future of AI in digital wellness holds immense potential for creating personalized, effective, and engaging health management solutions. However, it is crucial to address regulatory, ethical, and data privacy concerns to ensure these technologies are safe and beneficial for all users.

Chapter 12: Practical Solutions for Digital Wellness:

As our digital lives become increasingly intertwined with our daily routines, implementing practical solutions for digital wellness is crucial. This chapter explores actionable strategies to promote a healthier relationship with technology in various aspects of life.

Workplace Digital Wellness

1. Time Management Apps:
   - Utilize apps like RescueTime to analyze online time usage and block distracting websites.
   - Google's Digital Wellbeing app for Android helps monitor and limit app usage.

2. Preventing Eyestrain:
   - Implement blue light filtering apps like F.lux or Eye Pro to reduce eye fatigue.
   - Use the 20-20-20 rule: Every 20 minutes, look at something 20 feet away for 20 seconds.

3. Mindfulness and Well-being Apps:
   - Incorporate apps like Headspace for guided meditation sessions.
   - Use habit-forming apps like Streaks to establish healthy digital routines.

4. Establish Digital Boundaries:
   - Set clear work hours and stick to them, especially for remote workers.
   - Create "no-device" zones or times in the workplace.

Personal Digital Wellness

1. Digital Detox Periods:
   - Implement regular "digital detox" periods to disconnect from technology.
   - Use features like "Do Not Disturb" or "Focus" modes on devices.

2. Mindful Social Media Usage:
   - Set time limits for social media apps.
   - Regularly audit and curate social media feeds to ensure a positive experience.

3. Physical Activity Integration:
   - Use apps like Wakeout for quick, 30-second workouts throughout the day.
   - Incorporate standing desks or walking meetings to reduce sedentary behavior.

4. Sleep Hygiene:
   - Avoid screens at least an hour before bedtime.
   - Use night mode settings on devices to reduce blue light exposure in the evening.

Family and Education

1. Modeling Good Behavior:
   - Set a positive example by limiting device use during family time.
   - Demonstrate responsible social media practices.

2. Digital Literacy Education:
   - Teach children about online safety, privacy, and responsible digital citizenship.
   - Use resources from organizations like Common Sense Education for age-appropriate digital literacy lessons.

3. Balanced Technology Use:
   - Establish family guidelines for screen time and device usage.
   - Encourage a mix of online and offline activities.

Organizational Strategies

1. AI-Powered Wellness Programs:
   - Implement AI-driven personalized wellness programs for employees.
   - Use AI analytics to detect signs of stress or burnout and offer support.

2. Continuous Learning Culture:
   - Provide training on new digital tools and technologies to reduce tech-related stress.
   - Foster a culture of adaptability and innovation.

3. Accessibility Considerations:
   - Leverage AI to improve digital accessibility for employees with disabilities.
   - Ensure all digital tools and platforms are inclusive and user-friendly.

By implementing these practical solutions, individuals, families, and organizations can foster a healthier relationship with technology, leading to improved well-being, productivity, and overall digital wellness. The key is to find a balance that works for each unique situation and to remain flexible as technology and our digital lives continue to evolve.

Creating a balanced digital diet:

Creating a balanced digital diet is essential for maintaining mental health and overall well-being in our increasingly connected world. Here are practical strategies to help individuals and families establish a healthy relationship with technology:

1. Follow Reliable News Sources
- Choose trustworthy outlets: Ensure that the news you consume comes from credible sources, such as established news organizations (e.g., BBC, The Guardian).
- Verify information: Before sharing news, especially from social media or friends, double-check its accuracy against reliable sites.

2. Manage Screen Time
- Set limits: Create personal or family guidelines for screen time, such as "Screen-Free Saturdays" or specific hours when devices are put away.
- Use built-in tools: Utilize smartphone features like Apple's Screen Time or Android's Digital Wellbeing to monitor and limit usage.

3. Support Development and Interaction
- Create tech-free moments: Establish times during meals or family activities when devices are not allowed to encourage face-to-face interaction.
- Limit screen exposure for young children: Follow guidelines to restrict screen time for infants and toddlers, as excessive exposure can hinder development.

4. Incorporate Mindfulness and Relaxation
- Mindfulness apps: Use apps like Headspace or Calm to integrate mindfulness practices into your daily routine, helping to reduce stress and improve focus.
- Engage in offline activities: Encourage hobbies that do not involve screens, such as reading, crafting, or spending time outdoors.

5. Set Digital Boundaries
- Establish "no-phone" zones: Designate areas in the home where devices are not allowed, such as the dining room or bedrooms.
- Create a digital media use agreement: Work with family members to set rules and expectations around technology use, ensuring everyone is on the same page.

6. Monitor and Reflect on Usage
- Track time spent online: Use apps like RescueTime to analyze how much time is spent on different activities and identify areas for improvement.
- Ask reflective questions: Regularly evaluate how digital usage affects mood, sleep, and social interactions. Consider whether certain activities lead to stress or anxiety.

7. Educate About Digital Citizenship
- Teach responsible use: Educate children and teens about online safety, privacy, and the importance of respectful communication in digital spaces.
- Promote critical thinking: Encourage discussions about the content consumed online, helping young users develop the skills to evaluate information critically.

8. Balance Digital and Real-World Interactions
- Prioritize face-to-face connections: Foster relationships by spending quality time with friends and family without the distraction of devices.
- Encourage community engagement: Participate in local events or activities that promote social interaction and reduce reliance on digital communication.

By implementing these strategies, individuals and families can create a balanced digital diet that promotes healthy technology use, enhances well-being, and fosters meaningful connections in both digital and real-world environments.

Digital detox strategies and retreats:

Digital detox strategies and retreats are increasingly popular as individuals seek to reclaim their time and mental well-being from the overwhelming presence of technology. Here are some effective strategies for conducting a digital detox, as well as insights into retreats designed for this purpose:

Digital Detox Strategies

1. Turn Off Non-Essential Notifications:

- Disable notifications from non-essential apps to reduce distractions and interruptions throughout the day. This helps create a more focused environment and minimizes the urge to check devices constantly.

2. Designate Device-Free Zones:
  - Create specific areas in your home where devices are not allowed, such as the dining room or bedroom. This encourages more meaningful interactions and helps establish boundaries between digital and personal life.

3. Limit Device Usage:
  - Commit to using only one device at a time. For example, avoid multitasking with a phone while watching TV. This practice can enhance concentration and presence in the moment.

4. Schedule Internet Time Outs:
  - Set aside specific times during the day for internet use, allowing for breaks to disconnect and engage in offline activities. This can help manage screen time and reduce dependency on digital devices.

5. Conduct a Digital Audit:
  - Review your apps and digital habits. Uninstall or remove distracting apps and limit access to those that do not contribute positively to your life. This can help streamline your digital experience and reduce unnecessary screen time.

6. Use Airplane Mode:
  - Utilize airplane mode during designated times to block calls and notifications while still allowing access to offline content, such as music or downloaded documents.

7. Engage in Nature and Offline Activities:
  - Spend time outdoors or engage in hobbies that do not involve screens. This can help recharge your mental health and provide a refreshing break from technology.

Digital Detox Retreats

1. Wellness Retreats:
  - Many wellness retreats offer programs specifically designed to facilitate digital detoxes. These retreats often provide a technology-free environment where participants can focus on mindfulness, relaxation, and self-care.

2. Structured Programs:
   - Retreats may include structured activities such as yoga, meditation, hiking, and workshops that promote self-reflection and connection with nature, allowing participants to disconnect from their devices and reconnect with themselves.

3. Community Support:
   - Attending a retreat provides a sense of community and shared experience, as participants often engage in discussions about their digital habits and learn from each other's journeys toward better digital wellness.

4. Guided Detox Experiences:
   - Some retreats offer guided detox experiences, including mindfulness training and workshops on managing technology use effectively upon returning to daily life.

Benefits of Digital Detox

- Improved Mental Health: Taking a break from technology can reduce stress, anxiety, and feelings of overwhelm associated with constant connectivity.

- Enhanced Focus and Productivity: Reducing distractions allows for improved concentration and productivity in both personal and professional tasks.

- Better Sleep Quality: Disconnecting from screens, especially before bedtime, can lead to improved sleep quality by reducing blue light exposure.

- Stronger Relationships: Spending quality time with family and friends without the interference of devices can strengthen personal connections.

By implementing these strategies and considering retreats focused on digital detox, individuals can cultivate a healthier relationship with technology, ultimately enhancing their mental well-being and quality of life.

Ergonomic setups for different devices:

Creating ergonomic setups for different devices is essential for promoting comfort, productivity, and overall well-being while using technology. Here's a detailed guide on how to set up ergonomic workstations for various devices:

1. Desktop Computer Setup

- Chair: Use an ergonomic chair that provides lumbar support. Adjust the height so that your feet rest flat on the ground or on a footrest, with your knees at or slightly below hip level.

- Desk Height: Ensure your desk is at a height that allows your arms to be parallel to the floor when typing. If the desk is too high, consider using a chair with adjustable height or a footrest.

- Monitor Placement: Position your monitor about an arm's length away, with the top of the screen at or slightly below eye level. This helps prevent neck strain.

- Keyboard and Mouse: Place your keyboard close enough to your body so that your wrists can rest flat or slightly tilted downwards. Your elbows should be at a 90-degree angle. Use a mouse that fits comfortably in your hand and allows your wrist to remain in a neutral position.

- Lighting: Ensure adequate lighting to reduce glare on your screen and minimize eye strain. Use natural light when possible or a desk lamp that simulates daylight.

2. Laptop Setup

- External Accessories: Since laptops often have low screens and cramped keyboards, consider using an external keyboard and mouse. This allows for better positioning and reduces strain.

- Laptop Stand: Use a laptop stand to raise the screen to eye level. This helps maintain a neutral neck position.

- Posture: Sit up straight with your shoulders relaxed. Keep your elbows close to your body, and avoid hunching over the laptop.

- Breaks: Take regular breaks to stretch and move around to prevent stiffness and fatigue.

3. Tablet Setup

- Support: Use a stand to hold your tablet at eye level. This prevents neck strain and allows for a more comfortable viewing angle.

- Keyboard: If you use a keyboard with your tablet, ensure it is positioned so that your wrists are straight and your elbows are at a comfortable angle.

- Posture: Keep your back supported and avoid leaning forward. Consider using a cushion or a chair with good back support.

4. Mobile Phone Setup

- Hand Position: Hold your phone at eye level to avoid bending your neck down. Use a pop socket or grip to reduce strain on your fingers.

- Voice Commands: Utilize voice commands or dictation features to minimize the need for typing.

- Breaks: Limit continuous phone use and take breaks to prevent eye strain and hand fatigue.

5. General Ergonomic Tips

- Frequent Breaks: Implement the 20-20-20 rule: every 20 minutes, look at something 20 feet away for 20 seconds to reduce eye strain.

- Stretching: Incorporate stretching exercises into your routine to alleviate tension and improve circulation.

- Hydration: Keep water nearby to stay hydrated, which can help maintain energy levels and focus.

By following these ergonomic setup guidelines for different devices, individuals can significantly reduce the risk of discomfort and injury while enhancing productivity and well-being in their digital environments.

Eye exercises and vision care:

Based on the search results, here's an overview of eye exercises and vision care:

Common Eye Exercises

1. The 20-20-20 Rule:
   - Every 20 minutes, look at something 20 feet away for 20 seconds.
   - This helps reduce digital eye strain for those who work with computers.

2. Focus Change:
   - Hold a finger a few inches from your eye and focus on it.
   - Slowly move the finger away, maintaining focus.
   - Look at a distant object, then back to your finger.

3. Near and Far Focus:
   - Focus on your thumb 10 inches from your face for 15 seconds.
   - Then focus on an object 20 feet away for 15 seconds.
   - Repeat several times.

4. Figure Eight:
   - Trace an imaginary figure eight with your eyes.
   - Do this for 30 seconds, then switch directions.

5. Eye Movements:
   - Close your eyes and slowly move them up, down, left, and right.

6. Palming:
   - Rub your hands together to warm them.
   - Close your eyes and place your palms over them for 5 minutes.

7. Blinking:
   - Consciously blink to help restore the tear film and reduce dry eyes.

Benefits and Limitations

- Eye exercises can help with digital eye strain, focusing issues, and certain eye movement conditions.

- They may be beneficial for conditions like convergence insufficiency, strabismus, and amblyopia.
- However, eye exercises are not proven to improve vision for refractive errors like myopia, hyperopia, or astigmatism.
- They are also unlikely to help with eye diseases such as glaucoma, cataracts, or macular degeneration.

Vision Therapy

- Vision therapy is a more comprehensive approach prescribed by eye care professionals.
- It may include eye exercises along with special lenses, prisms, patches, or other tools3.
- Vision therapy can be effective for specific conditions involving eye alignment and focusing.

General Eye Health Tips

1. Get regular comprehensive eye exams.
2. Wear sunglasses to protect from UV rays.
3. Maintain a healthy diet rich in antioxidants and vitamin A.
4. Wear prescribed corrective lenses as needed.
5. Consider quitting smoking for better eye health.

While eye exercises can be beneficial for certain conditions and for reducing eye strain, they are not a substitute for professional eye care. It's important to consult with an eye care professional for any vision concerns or before starting an eye exercise regimen.

Posture improvement techniques:

Improving posture is essential for overall health and well-being, especially in today's world where many people spend prolonged hours sitting at desks or using devices. Here are effective techniques and exercises to enhance posture:

General Posture Improvement Techniques

1. Mindfulness of Posture:
   - Regularly check in with your posture throughout the day. Be aware of how you hold your body while sitting, standing, or walking.

2. Ergonomic Workstation Setup:
   - Adjust your chair, desk, and computer screen to promote good posture. The screen should be at eye level, and your chair should support your lower back.

3. Proper Sitting Position:
   - Sit with your back straight, shoulders relaxed, and feet flat on the floor. Avoid crossing your legs, and keep your knees at a right angle.

4. Standing Posture:
   - Stand tall with your feet shoulder-width apart. Keep your shoulders back, and pull your stomach in. Your head should be level, and arms should hang naturally at your sides.

5. Regular Breaks:
   - Take breaks every 30 minutes to stand, stretch, and move around. This helps prevent stiffness and encourages better posture.

6. Footwear:
   - Wear comfortable shoes with good arch support. Avoid high heels, which can alter your center of gravity and lead to poor posture.

Exercises for Posture Improvement

1. Bridges:
   - Strengthen glutes and lower back.
   - Lie on your back with knees bent. Lift hips toward the ceiling, hold for a few seconds, and lower back down. Repeat 10-15 times.

2. Plank Pose:
   - Strengthens core, shoulders, and back.
   - Hold a plank position on your forearms and toes, keeping your body in a straight line for 20-60 seconds.

3. Cat-Cow Stretch:
   - Promotes spinal flexibility.
   - On all fours, alternate between arching your back (cat) and dipping it (cow) while breathing deeply.

4. Child's Pose:
  - Stretches the back and hips.
  - Sit on your shins, fold forward, and extend your arms in front of you, relaxing in the pose for several breaths.

5. Shoulder Blade Squeeze:
  - Strengthens upper back muscles.
  - Sit or stand with arms at your sides. Squeeze your shoulder blades together and hold for a few seconds, then release. Repeat 10 times.

6. Wall Angels:
  - Improves shoulder mobility and posture.
  - Stand with your back against a wall, arms raised in a "W" position. Slide your arms up to form a "Y" and back down, keeping contact with the wall.

7. Stretching:
  - Incorporate stretches for the chest, shoulders, and back to relieve tension and improve flexibility. Examples include doorway stretches and upper back stretches.

Additional Tips

- Stay Active: Engage in regular physical activity, including cardio, strength training, and flexibility exercises.
- Maintain a Healthy Weight: Excess weight can strain your back and negatively impact posture.
- Seek Professional Help: If you experience persistent discomfort or pain, consider consulting a physical therapist or ergonomics expert for personalized guidance.

By incorporating these techniques and exercises into your daily routine, you can significantly improve your posture, reduce discomfort, and enhance overall health and productivity.

Mindfulness and meditation in the digital age:

Mindfulness and meditation have taken on new importance in the digital age as tools to help manage the challenges of constant connectivity and information overload. Here are some key points about practicing mindfulness and meditation in our digital world:

1. Digital mindfulness practices:
   - Using meditation apps and online guided sessions to develop a regular practice
   - Setting reminders on devices to take mindful breaks throughout the day
   - Practicing mindful use of technology, being intentional about when and how we engage
with devices

2. Benefits in the digital context:
   - Reducing stress and anxiety related to information overload and constant notifications
   - Improving focus and attention span in the face of digital distractions
   - Enhancing self-awareness of digital habits and their impact on wellbeing

3. Integrating mindfulness with technology:
   - Using wearables and biofeedback devices to track physiological markers of stress and
relaxation
   - Leveraging AI and machine learning to provide personalized mindfulness
recommendations
   - Creating "digital sanctuaries" - designated times and spaces free from devices

4. Addressing digital-specific challenges:
   - Practicing "uni-tasking" instead of multitasking across multiple digital platforms
   - Being mindful of social media use and its effects on mental health
   - Using mindfulness to combat "technostress" and digital burnout

5. Mindful communication in the digital sphere:
   - Bringing full attention and presence to digital interactions
   - Practicing empathy and compassion in online communications
   - Taking pauses before responding to emotionally-charged digital content

6. Balancing online and offline mindfulness:
   - Complementing digital practices with in-person meditation groups or retreats
   - Engaging in nature-based mindfulness practices as a counterpoint to screen time
   - Finding a personal balance between using supportive technologies and unplugging
completely

By adapting traditional mindfulness and meditation practices to the digital context,
individuals can cultivate greater awareness, balance, and wellbeing in their technology-
infused lives. The key is to use digital tools mindfully while also creating space for
disconnection and presence in the physical world.

Chapter 13: Digital Wellness Across Generations:

The digital landscape affects different age groups in unique ways, requiring tailored approaches to digital wellness. This chapter explores how various generations interact with technology and strategies to promote digital well-being across age groups.

Generation Z: The Digital Natives

Generation Z, born into a world of ubiquitous technology, faces distinct challenges:

1. Seamless Integration of Technology:
   - Gen Z effortlessly blends screens into all aspects of life, from socializing to learning and working.

2. Challenges:
   - Risk of excessive screen time and social media addiction.
   - Potential for decreased face-to-face social skills.

3. Digital Wellness Strategies:
   - Encourage purposeful screen time and set limits on social media consumption.
   - Promote digital detoxes and offline activities to balance digital experiences.
   - Foster critical thinking skills to navigate online information and relationships.

Millennials and Generation X: The Digital Adapters

These generations have witnessed the transition from analog to digital:

1. Balanced Approach:
   - Value both face-to-face interactions and digital convenience.
   - More likely to remember life before pervasive digital technology.

2. Digital Wellness Focus:
   - Create designated screen-free zones at home.
   - Prioritize outdoor activities and non-digital hobbies.
   - Practice mindful use of technology, being intentional about engagement.

3. Leveraging Health Tech:
   - Embrace wearable devices and health apps for fitness tracking and wellness management.
   - Utilize telemedicine platforms for convenient healthcare access.

Baby Boomers: Embracing the Digital Age

Baby Boomers approach technology with a mix of curiosity and caution:

1. Digital Adoption:
   - Increasingly using screens for communication, hobbies, and information access.
   - May find aspects of the digital world overwhelming.

2. Digital Wellness Strategies:
   - Provide workshops on digital literacy and online safety.
   - Emphasize the benefits of video calls for maintaining social connections.
   - Encourage gradual integration of technology into daily life.

Silent Generation: Navigating New Terrain

The oldest generation may be more hesitant to engage with digital technology:

1. Technology Engagement:
   - Some embrace screens for communication and entertainment, while others prefer traditional interactions.

2. Digital Wellness Approach:
   - Offer personalized support in setting up and using devices.
   - Showcase the value of online communities for staying connected.
   - Ensure technology enhances quality of life without causing frustration.

Cross-Generational Digital Wellness Initiatives

1. Family Dialogues:
   - Encourage open conversations about digital habits and their impact across generations.
   - Create opportunities for different age groups to share their perspectives on technology use.

2. Intergenerational Learning:
   - Facilitate workshops where younger generations can teach older ones about new technologies.
   - Encourage older generations to share wisdom about maintaining human connections in the digital age.

3. Collaborative Digital Detox:
   - Organize family or community events that promote offline activities and face-to-face interactions.

4. Mindfulness Practices:
   - Introduce mindfulness techniques adapted for different age groups to manage digital stress.
   - Emphasize the importance of being present and attentive in both digital and physical interactions.

By tailoring digital wellness strategies to each generation's unique needs and experiences, we can foster a healthier relationship with technology across all age groups. The key is to recognize the diverse perspectives on digital engagement and create inclusive approaches that benefit everyone in our increasingly connected world.

Children and screen time:

Here are some key points about children and screen time based on the search results:

1. Guidelines and recommendations:
- No screen time for children under 2 years old
- No more than 1 hour per day for children aged 2-5 years
- No more than 2 hours of recreational screen time per day for children aged 5-17 years (not including schoolwork)

2. Current usage:
- Most Australian children exceed recommended screen time limits
- Only 15-23% of children meet the guidelines
- Screen time tends to increase between ages 10-14, especially for boys

3. Potential negative effects of excessive screen time:
- Delayed development in young children, especially in communication and problem-solving skills
- Lower language and cognitive test scores
- Structural brain changes in some cases
- Behavioral problems, anxiety, lower self-esteem
- Obesity and poor diet
- Sleep disturbances
- Reduced physical activity
- Impaired social-emotional development

4. Contextual factors that matter:
- Content of screen media
- Whether screens are used interactively
- If parents co-view and engage with children
- Background TV exposure
- Overall family media habits

5. Potential benefits of appropriate use:
- Educational content can support learning
- Some games may help with stress management skills
- Video calls can maintain social connections

6. Recommendations for parents:
- Set time limits and stick to them
- Choose age-appropriate, high-quality content
- Co-view and engage with children during screen time
- Encourage alternative activities like reading and outdoor play
- Model healthy screen habits
- Keep screens out of bedrooms

7. Need for more research:
- More longitudinal studies are needed to understand long-term impacts
- Effects likely depend on many factors beyond just time spent on screens

The key is finding an appropriate balance and being mindful of how screens are used, rather than viewing all screen time as inherently negative. Parental involvement and setting healthy boundaries are important.

Teenagers and social media:

Based on the search results, here are key points about teenagers and social media:

1. Usage statistics:
- 97% of teens say they use the internet daily
- YouTube is the most popular platform, used by 95% of teens
- TikTok (67%), Instagram (62%), and Snapchat (59%) are also widely used
- Facebook usage has declined sharply among teens, from 71% in 2014-15 to 32% now

2. Frequency of use:
- 35% of teens say they use at least one major platform "almost constantly"
- 19% use YouTube almost constantly, 16% for TikTok, and 15% for Snapchat

3. Demographic differences:
- Teen boys are more likely to use YouTube, Twitch, and Reddit
- Teen girls are more likely to use TikTok, Instagram, and Snapchat
- Black and Hispanic teens report higher usage of TikTok, Instagram, Twitter, and
WhatsApp compared to White teens

4. Potential benefits:
- Staying connected with friends and family
- Finding support networks
- Self-expression and creativity
- Access to information and educational content

5. Potential risks:
- Excessive screen time linked to mental health issues
- Exposure to harmful content or cyberbullying
- Privacy and safety concerns
- Sleep disruption
- Negative impact on self-esteem and body image

6. Impact on mental health:
- Effects vary among individuals
- Some studies link heavy use (3+ hours daily) to higher risk of mental health issues
- Content type matters - certain content may increase risks for vulnerable teens

7. Parental guidance:
- Set rules and limits on usage
- Monitor accounts, especially for younger teens
- Educate about responsible use and online safety
- Model good digital habits
- Encourage offline activities and face-to-face interactions

8. Brain development:
- Teen brains are in a sensitive period for identity formation
- Social media may affect emotional learning, impulse control, and emotional regulation

Overall, while social media offers benefits for teens, it also presents risks that require parental awareness, education, and guidance to ensure healthy usage.

Adults balancing work and personal digital use:

Adults balancing work and personal digital use face several challenges in the digital age. Here are key points to consider:

1. Blurred boundaries:
  - The lines between work and personal life have become increasingly blurred due to technological advancements.
  - Mobile devices and digital tools allow work to extend beyond traditional office hours and spaces.

2. Flexibility and autonomy:
  - Digital technology enables more flexible working arrangements, potentially supporting better work-life balance.
  - However, the impact depends on how this flexibility is implemented and the level of worker autonomy.

3. Work-life spillover:
  - Despite increased flexibility, ICT workers report only slightly higher satisfaction with work-life fit compared to other sectors.
  - Technology can create pressure to be constantly available, making it difficult to disconnect from work.

4. Mindful technology use:
  - Practicing mindfulness can help adults manage digital stress and create intentional boundaries.
  - Mindful approaches include setting limits on device use, practicing digital detoxes, and being more intentional about digital consumption4.

5. Productivity and focus:
  - Mindfulness techniques can enhance productivity by encouraging focused attention on single tasks, countering the multitasking tendencies encouraged by digital environments.

6. Communication:
  - Mindful communication in digital spaces can foster more meaningful connections and reduce misunderstandings.

7. Stress management:
  - Regular mindfulness practices, such as meditation or breathing exercises, can help manage stress related to constant connectivity.

8. Technology as a solution:
  - Paradoxically, technology itself can be leveraged to promote better digital habits, with apps offering mindfulness exercises and digital wellbeing tools.

To effectively balance work and personal digital use, adults should:
- Set clear boundaries between work and personal time
- Practice mindful technology use
- Utilize digital tools that promote wellbeing and productivity
- Regularly disconnect and engage in offline activities
- Be aware of the potential for work to encroach on personal time and vice versa
- Communicate expectations clearly with employers and colleagues regarding availability outside of work hours

By implementing these strategies, adults can work towards a healthier relationship with technology that supports both their professional and personal lives.

Seniors embracing technology safely:

Seniors embracing technology safely involves understanding both the benefits and challenges they face, and implementing strategies to ensure a positive and secure experience. Here are some insights and tips based on the search results:

Benefits of Technology for Seniors

1. Improved Communication and Social Connections:
   - Technology enables seniors to stay connected with family and friends through video calls and social media, helping to combat loneliness and social isolation.

2. Access to Healthcare Resources:
   - Telemedicine and health-monitoring devices allow seniors to manage health conditions more effectively from home, reducing the need for frequent in-person visits.

3. Enhanced Independence and Safety:
   - Smart home technologies, such as voice-activated assistants and automated controls, help seniors manage daily tasks and enhance safety with features like fall detection sensors.

4. Cognitive Stimulation and Lifelong Learning:
   - Engaging with technology through online courses, educational apps, and brain-training games can promote cognitive health and lifelong learning.

5. Convenient Access to Services:
   - Online platforms provide easy access to shopping, banking, and entertainment, making everyday tasks more convenient.

Challenges and Solutions

1. Fear of Technology:
   - Seniors may feel intimidated by new devices and platforms. Starting with user-friendly devices and taking small steps can help build confidence.

2. Physical Limitations:
   - Devices with larger text sizes, voice commands, and screen readers can assist those with vision, hearing, or mobility challenges.

3. Security Concerns:
  - Seniors should use strong, unique passwords, be cautious with personal information, and regularly update software to protect against scams and security threats.

4. Rapid Technological Change:
  - The fast pace of technology can be overwhelming. Seniors can benefit from tech literacy resources, such as online tutorials and community workshops, to stay informed and confident.

Tips for Safe Technology Use

1. Start with Simplicity:
  - Choose devices designed with simplicity in mind, such as smartphones with larger buttons and intuitive interfaces.

2. Leverage Built-in Features:
  - Utilize accessibility features and voice assistants to make technology more accessible and user-friendly.

3. Regular Practice:
  - Encourage regular use and exploration of devices to build familiarity and proficiency.

4. Seek Support:
  - Family members and tech-savvy friends can provide guidance and troubleshooting help.

5. Stay Informed:
  - Keep up with the latest security practices and be aware of common scams targeting seniors.

By embracing these strategies, seniors can safely and confidently integrate technology into their lives, enhancing their independence, health, and social connections. The goal is to bridge the digital divide by making technology accessible and beneficial for older adults.

Chapter 14: Cultural Perspectives on Digital Wellness:

Digital wellness is a multifaceted concept that varies significantly across cultures, influenced by diverse social norms, beliefs, and values. This chapter explores how cultural perspectives shape digital wellness practices and the importance of culturally adapting digital health interventions.

Cultural Adaptation of Digital Health Interventions

1. Importance of Cultural Context:
   - Digital health interventions must be responsive to the cultural and socioeconomic contexts of their intended audiences to be effective.
   - Cultural adaptation involves modifying interventions to align with the target audience's cultural norms, beliefs, and values.

2. Approaches to Cultural Adaptation:
   - The process includes designing culturally appropriate user interfaces and translating content to be accessible and meaningful.
   - Frameworks like the cultural sensitivity framework and ecological validity model guide these adaptations.

3. Challenges and Considerations:
   - Cultural adaptations require time, resources, and a deep understanding of the target group's relationship with technology.
   - Engaging a broad range of stakeholders, including community leaders and experts, is crucial for successful adaptation.

Cultural Influences on Digital Wellness

1. Cultural Differences in Technology Use:
   - Cultural elements such as individualism, contextuality, and time perception impact how different groups interact with technology.
   - For example, collectivist cultures may prefer digital health interventions that include peer-sharing options.

2. Health Perception and Communication:
  - Culture influences how health information is perceived and communicated, affecting the appropriateness of digital interventions.
  - Understanding these cultural nuances is essential for designing effective digital wellness programs.

3. Mindfulness and Digital Wellness:
  - Mindfulness, rooted in ancient contemplative practices, offers a universal approach to managing digital stress across cultures.
  - It encourages individuals to reassess their relationship with digital devices, fostering a more conscious and intentional approach.

Generational Perspectives on Digital Wellness

1. Digital Natives (Generation Z):
  - Raised amidst rapid technological advancement, they integrate screens into all aspects of life.
  - Digital wellness for this group involves setting limits on social media and engaging in digital detoxes.

2. Generation X and Millennials:
  - These generations bridge the gap between analog and digital, valuing both face-to-face interactions and digital convenience.
  - Strategies include creating screen-free zones and prioritizing offline activities.

3. Baby Boomers and the Silent Generation:
  - These older generations may approach technology with caution but increasingly use it to stay connected and informed.
  - Promoting digital literacy and online safety can empower them to embrace digital wellness confidently.

Cultural perspectives play a crucial role in shaping digital wellness practices. By understanding and respecting these cultural differences, digital health interventions can be more effectively tailored to meet the diverse needs of global populations. This approach not only enhances the reach and engagement of digital wellness programs but also helps bridge the digital divide, ensuring that all cultural groups can benefit from technological advancements in health and well-being.

Variations in digital use across English-speaking countries:

Based on the search results provided, there isn't specific information directly comparing digital use across English-speaking countries. However, I can synthesize some relevant insights about variations in digital use that may apply to English-speaking countries:

1. Language and content diversity:
- Despite English being dominant on the web (63.6% of top websites), there are still variations in how English is used online across different countries and cultures.
- English-speaking countries may have less need for translation tools compared to non-English speaking countries. The search results indicate that people in predominantly English-speaking countries are less likely to use online translation tools.

2. Adoption of new terminology:
- English-speaking countries may adopt new digital terminology at different rates. For example, terms like "story" for social media features may be adopted faster by younger generations.
- There may be variations in how quickly new internet slang or abbreviations are adopted across different English-speaking cultures.

3. Influence of other languages:
- In multilingual English-speaking countries (e.g., Canada with French, South Africa with multiple official languages), there may be more mixing of languages in digital communication.
- Exposure to diverse English dialects online (e.g., Indian English, African American Vernacular English) may influence digital language use differently across English-speaking countries.

4. Cultural context in digital health:
- The cultural adaptation of digital health interventions suggests that even among English-speaking countries, there may be a need to tailor digital health tools to specific cultural contexts.
- Socioeconomic factors within English-speaking countries could impact access to and use of digital technologies.

5. Social media platform preferences:
- While not specific to English-speaking countries, the search results suggest that different demographics may prefer different social media platforms. This could vary across English-speaking countries based on local trends and cultural preferences.

6. Digital literacy and age demographics:
- Variations in digital literacy levels and age demographics across English-speaking countries could lead to differences in how digital technologies are used and adopted.

While these points are not definitive comparisons, they suggest areas where variations in digital use might occur across English-speaking countries, based on cultural, linguistic, and socioeconomic factors.

Cultural influences on digital habits and wellness:

Based on the search results, here are some key points about cultural influences on digital habits and wellness:

1. Cultural impact on social media usage:
  - Culture influences how people use social networks and engage in online communities.
  - Different cultural groups may prefer different types of social media platforms or features based on their cultural norms and values.

2. Cultural adaptation of digital health interventions:
  - Digital health tools need to be culturally adapted to be effective for diverse populations.
  - This involves modifying content, user interfaces, and features to align with cultural norms, beliefs, and values of the target audience.
  - Cultural adaptation goes beyond simple translation and includes considering socioeconomic factors, literacy levels, and cultural contexts.

3. Generational differences:
  - Different generations have varying approaches to digital technology use, influenced by their cultural and technological upbringing.
  - Generation Z, as digital natives, integrates technology seamlessly into all aspects of life, while older generations may be more cautious.

4. Language and accessibility:
  - Language barriers can significantly impact the use of digital health tools among culturally and linguistically diverse populations.
  - Providing content in multiple languages and using plain language principles can improve accessibility.

5. Cultural perceptions of health and technology:
  - Cultural beliefs about health, privacy, and technology use can influence how different groups engage with digital wellness tools.
  - Some cultures may prefer more community-oriented features, while others may value individual privacy.

6. Digital literacy and access:
  - Cultural and socioeconomic factors can affect digital literacy levels and access to technology.
  - This can create or exacerbate digital divides among different cultural groups.

7. Cultural humility in design:
  - Involving diverse stakeholders and community members in the design process can lead to more culturally appropriate digital wellness solutions.
  - A culturally humble approach recognizes the dynamic nature of culture and the need for ongoing adaptation.

8. Intersection of culture and context:
  - Cultural factors interact with other contextual elements like economic conditions and social systems, influencing how people use and benefit from digital wellness tools.

9. Tailoring user experiences:
  - Culturally adapted digital interventions may include features that address specific cultural needs, such as social support functions or culturally relevant content.

10. Evolving cultural norms:
  - The COVID-19 pandemic has influenced cultural consumption patterns, including increased engagement with online cultural content among younger generations.

These insights highlight the importance of considering cultural factors when designing, implementing, and promoting digital wellness initiatives to ensure they are effective and accessible across diverse populations.

Global best practices in digital wellness:

Based on the search results and the query for global best practices in digital wellness, here are some key points:

1. Cultural adaptation of digital health interventions:
  - Digital health tools and interventions should be culturally adapted to be effective for diverse populations globally.
  - This involves modifying content, user interfaces, and features to align with cultural norms, beliefs, and values of the target audience.
  - Consideration of socioeconomic factors, literacy levels, and cultural contexts is crucial.

2. Mindfulness and digital balance:
  - Mindfulness practices are gaining prominence as a tool to navigate the challenges of the digital era across cultures.
  - Encouraging focused attention and intentional use of technology can help manage digital stress and improve overall well-being.
  - Mindfulness apps and digital well-being tools are becoming popular globally as accessible ways to integrate mindfulness into daily life.

3. Workplace digital wellness:
  - Companies worldwide are addressing digital workplace challenges like application overload and digital noise pollution.
  - Employers are focusing on tools that increase concentration and overall well-being, such as meditation apps and task management software.
  - Creating supportive digital work environments that promote work-life balance is becoming a global trend.

4. Global strategy on digital health:
  - The WHO's Global Strategy on Digital Health 2020-2025 aims to strengthen health systems through digital technologies.
  - It emphasizes the importance of data security, privacy, and ethical considerations in digital health initiatives.
  - The strategy promotes health innovations and cutting-edge digital technologies while ensuring they are appropriate and accessible for all Member States.

5. Digital detox and boundaries:
   - Implementing regular "digital detox" periods is becoming a global best practice to disconnect from technology and reduce digital fatigue.
   - Setting clear boundaries between work and personal digital use is encouraged across cultures.

6. Promoting digital literacy:
   - Enhancing digital literacy skills is crucial for empowering individuals to use technology effectively and safely.
   - This includes education on online safety, privacy, and responsible digital citizenship.

7. Inclusive design:
   - Ensuring digital health solutions are accessible and user-friendly for all populations, including those with disabilities or limited access to technology.

8. Balancing innovation with ethical considerations:
   - As digital health technologies advance globally, there's an emphasis on balancing innovation with ethical considerations, data protection, and privacy.

These global best practices aim to promote digital wellness by addressing the challenges of the digital age while leveraging its benefits for health and well-being across diverse cultural contexts.

Chapter 15: Emerging Technologies and Future Trends:

As we look toward the future, emerging technologies are set to transform industries, societies, and individual lives in profound ways. This chapter explores the key technological trends that are shaping the future and their potential impacts.

Key Emerging Technologies

1. Artificial Intelligence (AI) and AI-Generated Content:
   - AI continues to evolve, with applications expanding into content generation, where AI models like GPT and DALL-E create high-quality text, images, and videos. This democratizes content creation and reduces costs, enabling small businesses and individuals to produce content at scale.

2. Quantum Computing:
   - Quantum computing leverages quantum mechanics to process information much faster than traditional computers. It holds potential for breakthroughs in fields like cryptography and drug discovery, although it is still in the early stages of development.

3. 5G and Connectivity Technologies:
   - The expansion of 5G networks promises faster data speeds and more stable connections, facilitating transformative technologies such as IoT, augmented reality, and autonomous vehicles. This is crucial for real-time communications and processing large data volumes with minimal delay.

4. Virtual Reality (VR) and Augmented Reality (AR):
   - VR and AR technologies are becoming more immersive and user-friendly, with applications in gaming, training, retail, and therapeutic contexts. These technologies enhance customer experiences and offer new ways to interact with digital content.

5. Internet of Things (IoT) and Smart Cities:
   - IoT involves integrating sensors and devices to manage resources efficiently in smart cities, improving traffic, energy use, and public safety. As urban areas grow, IoT helps manage complexities and enhance residents' quality of life.

6. Biotechnology and Agriculture:
   - Advances in biotechnology, such as CRISPR gene editing, are revolutionizing agriculture by developing crops with enhanced traits to withstand environmental stresses. This is crucial for adapting to climate change and ensuring food security.

7. Autonomous Vehicles:
   - Autonomous vehicles use AI and sensors to operate without human intervention. Progress is being made in integrating autonomy into public transportation and logistics, potentially reducing accidents and emissions.

Future Trends and Implications

1. Ubiquitous Integration:
   - Future technologies will seamlessly integrate into daily life, with smart homes, cars, and cities enhancing quality of life through autonomous operation.

2. Hyper-Personalization:
   - Advances in AI and data analytics will enable technologies to cater to individual preferences, from personalized healthcare to tailored educational experiences.

3. Sustainable and Ethical Innovations:
   - As environmental and ethical concerns grow, technologies will focus on climate-positive practices, such as renewable energy and circular economies.

4. Democratization of Technology:
   - Access to technology will become more widespread, breaking down barriers and enabling small enterprises and individuals to harness high-end tools.

5. Human-Machine Collaboration:
   - Future technologies will augment human capabilities, with AI and robotics working alongside humans to enhance productivity and creativity.

6. Resilience and Security:
   - As dependence on technology increases, robust security measures will be essential to protect users and data from threats.

These emerging technologies and trends present both opportunities and challenges. As we embrace these advancements, it is crucial to consider ethical implications, ensure equitable access, and focus on sustainable development to create a brighter, more inclusive future.

Virtual and Augmented Reality:

1. Applications across industries:
   - VR/AR are being used in diverse fields including education, healthcare, engineering, entertainment, architecture, and more.
   - Specific applications include medical training, engineering simulations, virtual tourism, mental health therapy, and immersive education.

2. Key technological components:
   - Computer vision, 3D mapping, sensors/cameras, haptic technology, and spatial audio are core technologies enabling VR/AR experiences.

3. Business impact:
   - VR/AR are revolutionizing business operations by enhancing training, streamlining design processes, and improving customer interactions.
   - Examples include Microsoft HoloLens for industrial training and remote assistance, and PTC Vuforia for machine maintenance and factory design.

4. Market growth:
   - The global VR/AR market is expected to reach $62 billion by 2029, with an annual growth rate of 8.97% from 2024-2029.

5. Immersive experiences:
   - VR provides fully simulated environments, while AR overlays digital information onto the real world.
   - Both technologies are creating more engaging and interactive experiences across various domains.

6. Healthcare applications:
   - VR is being used for medical training, surgical planning, and patient treatments.
   - AR assists in providing real-time information during surgeries and medical procedures.

7. Education and training:
   - VR/AR enable immersive learning experiences, allowing students to interact with 3D models and simulations.

- These technologies enhance comprehension and retention of complex concepts.

8. Entertainment and gaming:
  - VR continues to evolve in gaming, providing more immersive and interactive experiences.
  - AR is being used in live events, theme parks, and interactive entertainment experiences.

9. Challenges and considerations:
  - User comfort, motion sickness, and the need for high-quality content remain challenges for widespread adoption.
  - Privacy and security concerns need to be addressed as these technologies become more prevalent.

10. Future potential:
  - As VR/AR technologies advance, they are expected to play an increasingly significant role in how we work, learn, and interact with the world around us.

Internet of Things (IoT) and smart homes:

Based on the search results, here are key points about the Internet of Things (IoT) and smart homes:

1. Definition and concept:
  - IoT in smart homes refers to the interconnected network of devices and appliances that can communicate and be controlled remotely via the internet.
  - Smart homes use IoT technology to create intelligent living spaces that provide convenience, efficiency, and enhanced control.

2. Key technologies:
  - Smart sensors for detecting motion, temperature, humidity, and light
  - Voice assistants like Amazon Alexa or Google Assistant
  - Smart appliances that can communicate with a central hub
  - Security systems including cameras, door locks, and motion sensors
  - Energy management systems like smart thermostats and lighting

3. Applications:
  - Home automation for controlling lights, thermostats, and appliances

- Security and surveillance with real-time monitoring and alerts
- Energy efficiency through optimized usage of heating, cooling, and lighting
- Entertainment systems integration
- Health and well-being monitoring
- Home maintenance with predictive alerts

4. Benefits:
  - Increased convenience through remote control and automation
  - Enhanced security with real-time monitoring and alerts
  - Improved energy efficiency and cost savings
  - Personalization based on user preferences and habits
  - Accessibility features for individuals with disabilities

5. Challenges:
  - Data security and privacy concerns
  - Interoperability issues between devices from different manufacturers
  - Reliability and consistency of device performance
  - Initial costs of implementation
  - Need for user education and adaptation

6. Future trends:
  - Enhanced interconnectivity between devices
  - Integration of artificial intelligence for more intelligent automation
  - Expansion of the IoT ecosystem to cover more aspects of home living
  - Improved data security and privacy measures
  - Decreasing costs as technology becomes more widespread

7. Market growth:
  - The smart home market is expected to see significant growth, with projections
indicating a rise to $55.03 billion in the US market by 2028.

8. Popular IoT devices for smart homes:
  - Smart door locks and motion sensors
  - Smart kitchen appliances (refrigerators, ovens, coffee makers)
  - Smart thermostats and HVAC systems
  - Smart lighting systems
  - Voice-controlled assistants and hubs

The Internet of Things is transforming traditional homes into interconnected, intelligent living spaces that offer improved convenience, security, energy efficiency, and personalization. As the technology continues to evolve, we can expect even greater integration and sophistication in smart home systems.

Wearable technology and health tracking:

Wearable technology and health tracking devices have become increasingly popular and sophisticated in recent years. Here are some key points about this emerging technology:

1. Types of wearable health devices:
   - Fitness trackers (e.g. Fitbit, Garmin)
   - Smartwatches (e.g. Apple Watch, Samsung Galaxy Watch)
   - Smart clothing with embedded sensors
   - Wearable ECG monitors
   - Continuous glucose monitors
   - Smart patches for various health metrics

2. Common health metrics tracked:
   - Steps and physical activity
   - Heart rate and heart rhythm
   - Sleep patterns
   - Blood oxygen levels
   - Stress levels
   - Calories burned
   - Blood glucose (for some devices)

3. Key benefits:
   - Continuous health monitoring
   - Early detection of potential health issues
   - Empowering users to be more proactive about their health
   - Providing data to healthcare providers for better care
   - Motivating healthy behaviors and lifestyle changes

4. Emerging capabilities:
   - Integration of AI for predictive health analytics
   - More advanced biosensors for additional health metrics
   - Improved accuracy and clinical-grade measurements

- Enhanced connectivity with healthcare systems

5. Challenges:
   - Ensuring data privacy and security
   - Accuracy and reliability of measurements
   - User adoption and sustained engagement
   - Integration with existing healthcare workflows

6. Market growth:
   - The wearable health tech market is expanding rapidly
   - Major tech companies and startups are investing heavily in this space

7. Future trends:
   - More sophisticated and diverse wearable devices
   - Increased use in clinical settings and remote patient monitoring
   - Greater personalization of health insights and recommendations
   - Potential for wearables to assist in early disease detection

8. Considerations for users:
   - Choose devices that fit your specific health goals
   - Ensure compatibility with your smartphone/ecosystem
   - Consider battery life and comfort for long-term wear
   - Be aware of data privacy policies

As wearable health technology continues to advance, it has the potential to revolutionize personal health management and healthcare delivery by providing continuous, real-time health data and insights.

Preparing for future digital challenges:

1. Ensure robust connectivity:
   - Invest in sufficient bandwidth to support various devices and systems
   - Consider private LTE networks and 5G to enhance connectivity
   - Address connectivity challenges for remote sites

2. Evaluate organizational and technical readiness:
   - Assess if the organization believes in and is ready for change
   - Examine legacy IT systems and technical capabilities

- Ensure dedicated resources are committed to digital initiatives

3. Develop a comprehensive change management strategy:
   - Plan for organizational, process, behavioral, and cultural changes
   - Identify root causes of issues and build relationships with stakeholders
   - Use change management templates to guide the process

4. Address complexity and adoption challenges:
   - Seek out intuitive, integrated systems to minimize complexity
   - Provide comprehensive onboarding training for new tools
   - Offer continuous employee performance support to drive adoption

5. Take an incremental approach:
   - Start with small steps and build digital skills over time
   - Avoid aiming too high before the organization is ready
   - Recognize that digital transformation is an ongoing journey

6. Prepare for long-term evolution:
   - Understand that digital capabilities will need to change as technologies evolve
   - Be prepared for a continuous transformation process
   - Stay adaptable to keep pace with changing technologies

7. Focus on security and data privacy:
   - Address security concerns as organizations become more digitally exposed
   - Ensure robust security measures are in place to protect users and data

8. Align with sustainability goals:
   - Consider how digital initiatives can support carbon neutral and net zero targets
   - Integrate sustainability into digital transformation strategies

9. Foster a culture of innovation:
   - Encourage experimentation and learning from failures
   - Create an environment that supports continuous improvement

10. Develop digital skills:
   - Invest in training and development to address skill gaps
   - Consider partnerships or hiring to bring in necessary digital expertise

By focusing on these areas, organizations can better prepare themselves to navigate future digital challenges and opportunities in an increasingly technology-driven business landscape.

Chapter 16: Creating Your Personal Digital Wellness Plan:

In today's digital age, creating a personal digital wellness plan is essential for maintaining a healthy balance between technology use and overall well-being. This chapter provides a comprehensive guide to developing a digital wellness plan tailored to individual needs and preferences.

Understanding Digital Wellness

Digital wellness involves managing technology use to enhance well-being, productivity, and happiness. It requires self-awareness and intentional actions to ensure that technology serves as a tool for improvement rather than a source of distraction or stress.

Steps to Create Your Personal Digital Wellness Plan

1. Assess Your Current Digital Habits

- Reflect on Usage: Evaluate how you currently use technology. Consider the time spent on devices, the purpose of usage, and the impact on your daily life.
- Identify Patterns: Use tools like digital dashboards to understand your digital habits, including app usage and screen time.
- Self-Assessment: Consider how digital use affects your physical, mental, and emotional well-being.

2. Set SMART Goals

- Specific and Measurable: Define clear objectives, such as reducing screen time by 30 minutes daily or having tech-free meals.
- Achievable and Relevant: Ensure goals are realistic and align with your values and lifestyle.
- Time-Bound: Set deadlines to track progress and stay motivated.

3. Develop Actionable Strategies

- Focus Time with Tech: Be intentional about when and how you use technology. Prioritize tasks that require digital tools and eliminate unnecessary distractions.
- Unplug Regularly: Schedule regular digital detox periods to disconnect and recharge. This could include tech-free zones or times during the day.
- Minimize Distractions: Use features like "Do Not Disturb" to limit notifications and interruptions.

4. Incorporate Mindfulness and Self-Care

- Mindful Use: Practice mindfulness by being present during digital interactions. Avoid multitasking and focus on one task at a time.
- Self-Care Practices: Balance screen time with activities that promote relaxation and well-being, such as meditation, exercise, and spending time outdoors.

5. Monitor and Adjust Your Plan

- Regular Check-Ins: Periodically review your digital wellness plan to assess progress and make necessary adjustments.
- Stay Flexible: Be open to modifying your plan as your needs and circumstances change.

6. Foster a Supportive Environment

- Family and Community Engagement: Involve family members in creating healthy digital habits and discuss the importance of digital wellness together.
- Model Positive Behavior: Set an example for others by demonstrating responsible and mindful technology use.

Tools and Resources

- Digital Wellbeing Apps: Use apps designed to track and manage digital habits, providing insights and reminders to stay on track.
- Educational Resources: Access online courses and workshops to learn more about digital wellness practices and strategies.

By following these steps and leveraging available tools, individuals can create a personalized digital wellness plan that enhances their quality of life and fosters a healthier relationship with technology.

Assessing your current digital habits:

Based on the search results, here are some key steps for assessing your current digital habits:

1. Reflect on your usage:
- Evaluate how you currently use technology, including time spent on devices, purpose of usage, and impact on your daily life.
- Consider if you're using technology consciously or out of habit.
- Assess if screen time is taking away from other important activities like sleep, family time, etc.

2. Use tracking tools:
- Utilize digital wellbeing dashboards or apps that provide data on your app usage and screen time.
- Pay attention to how often you check your phone and use different apps throughout the day.

3. Conduct a self-assessment:
- Consider how your digital use affects your physical, mental, and emotional wellbeing.
- Evaluate if the content you consume online makes your life better.
- Assess if you're portraying your true self in your online contributions.

4. Take a digital wellbeing survey:
- Use surveys like the one mentioned in the search results to get a snapshot of how technology impacts key areas of your life, including:
  - Wellbeing
  - Boundaries
  - Communication
  - Focus
  - Connection
  - Purpose

5. Identify patterns:
- Look for patterns in your digital habits, such as checking email frequently or scrolling social media before bed.
- Notice any triggers that lead to excessive or unintended technology use.

6. Evaluate control and conscious usage:
- Assess whether you feel in control of your device usage or if it's controlling you.
- Consider if you're using technology mindfully or automatically.

7. Examine impact on relationships and productivity:
- Reflect on how your digital habits affect your interpersonal relationships.
- Consider whether technology is helping or hindering your efficiency and productivity.

8. Assess work-life balance:
- Evaluate if you feel pressure to be "always on" for work outside of working hours.
- Consider how your digital habits impact your work-life balance.

9. Review sleep habits:
- Examine how your technology use affects your sleep patterns.
- Consider if you delay sleep due to device use or check your phone first thing in the morning.

By thoroughly assessing these aspects of your digital habits, you can gain a comprehensive understanding of your current relationship with technology and identify areas for potential improvement.

Setting realistic goals:

Setting realistic goals for digital wellness is crucial for managing technology use in a way that enhances well-being and productivity. Here are some strategies to help you establish achievable and meaningful digital wellness goals:

1. Reflect on Your Current Digital Habits

- Assess Usage: Start by evaluating how much time you spend on various devices and platforms. Use tools or apps that track screen time to gain insights into your habits.

- Identify Patterns: Look for patterns in your usage, such as times of day when you tend to overuse technology or specific activities that lead to excessive screen time.

2. Define Clear Objectives

- Specific Goals: Set specific, measurable goals. For example, aim to reduce screen time by a certain percentage, limit social media usage to a specific time frame, or designate tech-free hours each day.
- Realistic Expectations: Ensure your goals are achievable given your lifestyle. For instance, if you currently spend four hours a day on social media, reducing it to one hour immediately may not be realistic. Instead, aim for a gradual reduction.

3. Use the SMART Criteria

- Specific: Clearly define what you want to achieve (e.g., "Limit social media use to 30 minutes per day").
- Measurable: Ensure you can track your progress (e.g., using app usage statistics).
- Achievable: Set goals that are attainable based on your current habits.
- Relevant: Align your goals with your overall well-being and lifestyle objectives.
- Time-Bound: Set deadlines for your goals (e.g., "Reduce screen time by 25% over the next month").

4. Create Actionable Steps

- Break Goals into Tasks: Divide larger goals into smaller, manageable tasks. For example, if your goal is to reduce screen time, start by designating specific times for checking your phone.
- Implement Tech-Free Zones: Establish areas in your home where technology is not allowed, such as the dining room or bedrooms, to encourage more face-to-face interactions.

5. Monitor Progress and Adjust

- Regular Check-Ins: Schedule weekly or monthly reviews to assess your progress toward your goals. Adjust your strategies if you find certain goals are too challenging or not effective.
- Celebrate Achievements: Acknowledge and reward yourself for reaching milestones, no matter how small. This reinforces positive behavior and encourages continued effort.

6. Involve Family and Friends

- Set Goals Together: If applicable, involve family members or friends in your digital wellness goals. This can create a supportive environment and foster accountability.
- Discuss Boundaries: Talk about digital habits with loved ones and agree on shared goals, such as tech-free family dinners or weekend digital detoxes.

7. Educate Yourself

- Seek Resources: Attend workshops or read articles on digital wellness to gain insights and strategies for managing technology use effectively.
- Stay Informed: Keep up with the latest research and trends in digital wellness to adapt your goals as needed.

By following these steps, you can set realistic and meaningful goals for your digital wellness journey, enhancing your relationship with technology and improving your overall well-being.

Implementing changes gradually:

Implementing changes gradually is a crucial approach to achieving long-term digital wellness. This method allows you to adapt to new habits without feeling overwhelmed. Here are some effective strategies for making gradual changes to your digital habits:

1. Start Small

- Focus on One Change at a Time: Instead of overhauling your entire digital routine at once, choose one specific change to focus on. For example, if you want to reduce screen time, start by limiting social media usage for a week.
- Set Mini-Goals: Break your larger goals into smaller, manageable tasks. For instance, if your goal is to reduce screen time by 30 minutes a day, aim to cut back by 5-10 minutes each week.

2. Create a Plan

- Outline Your Changes: Develop a clear plan detailing the changes you want to make, including specific actions and timelines. This helps you stay organized and focused.

- Use a Calendar: Mark your planned changes on a calendar to visualize your progress and keep track of your commitments.

3. Monitor Progress

- Track Your Habits: Use apps or journals to log your digital usage and monitor changes over time. This helps you stay accountable and identify patterns in your behavior.
- Reflect Regularly: Set aside time each week to reflect on your progress, noting successes and challenges. Adjust your approach as needed based on your reflections.

4. Gradually Increase Difficulty

- Build on Success: Once you successfully implement a small change, gradually increase the challenge. For example, if you've reduced social media time, consider adding tech-free periods during meals or before bedtime.
- Layer Changes: Introduce new habits one at a time, layering them on top of previous changes. This gradual approach prevents overwhelm and allows for smoother transitions.

5. Establish Routines

- Create Consistent Habits: Incorporate your changes into your daily routines. For example, designate specific times for checking emails or social media, and stick to those times to create structure.
- Use Reminders: Set reminders on your devices to prompt you to follow through with your new habits, such as turning off notifications during designated tech-free times.

6. Involve Others

- Share Your Goals: Discuss your digital wellness goals with family and friends. Their support can help you stay motivated and accountable.
- Engage in Group Activities: Consider participating in group activities that promote digital wellness, such as family game nights or outdoor excursions that encourage tech-free time.

7. Be Patient and Flexible

- Allow for Setbacks: Understand that setbacks are a normal part of the process. If you slip back into old habits, don't be too hard on yourself. Instead, reassess your approach and try again.

- Stay Adaptable: Be willing to adjust your goals and strategies as you learn what works best for you. Flexibility is key to finding a sustainable digital wellness routine.

8. Celebrate Milestones

- Acknowledge Progress: Celebrate small victories along the way to reinforce positive behavior. This could be as simple as treating yourself to something special or sharing your achievements with loved ones.
- Reflect on Benefits: As you implement changes, take note of the positive effects on your well-being, productivity, and relationships. This reflection can motivate you to continue making gradual improvements.

By implementing changes gradually, you can create a more balanced relationship with technology that enhances your digital wellness over time. This approach fosters sustainable habits and helps you adapt to new routines without feeling overwhelmed.

Monitoring progress and adjusting strategies:

Monitoring progress and adjusting strategies are essential components of maintaining and improving digital wellness. Here are key steps and considerations based on the search results:

1. Regular Check-Ins

- Schedule Assessments: Set regular intervals (weekly or monthly) to evaluate your digital habits and progress toward your wellness goals. This helps you stay accountable and allows for timely adjustments.

- Reflect on Experiences: Use these check-ins to reflect on what strategies have been effective and which have not. Consider how your digital habits impact your overall well-being, productivity, and relationships.

2. Gather Feedback

- Seek Input from Others: If you're part of a team or community, gather feedback from peers or family members about their observations regarding your digital habits. This can provide valuable insights into areas you may overlook.

- Create a Safe Space for Discussion: Encourage open discussions about digital wellness challenges within your community or workplace. Sharing experiences can help identify common issues and solutions.

3. Adjust Goals and Strategies

- Be Flexible with Goals: If you find certain goals are too ambitious or not challenging enough, adjust them to better fit your current situation. For example, if reducing social media usage by 50% feels unattainable, consider a smaller percentage.

- Implement New Strategies: Based on your reflections and feedback, introduce new techniques or tools to enhance your digital wellness. This might include new apps for tracking usage, mindfulness practices, or setting clearer boundaries.

4. Celebrate Milestones

- Acknowledge Progress: Recognizing and celebrating small victories can boost motivation. This could be as simple as noting a week of reduced screen time or successfully implementing tech-free periods.

- Share Success Stories: If you're part of a group, sharing success stories can inspire others and reinforce positive behaviors within the community.

5. Continuous Education

- Stay Informed: Keep up with the latest research and best practices in digital wellness. This can provide new insights and strategies to incorporate into your plan.

- Participate in Workshops: Attend digital wellness workshops or training sessions to learn from experts and gain practical tools for managing technology use effectively.

6. Utilize Technology Wisely

- Leverage Digital Tools: Use apps and tools designed to promote digital wellness, such as screen time trackers, focus apps, or mindfulness resources. These can help you monitor your habits and provide reminders to unplug.

Set up Notifications: Configure your devices to remind you to take breaks or engage in tech-free activities. This can help reinforce your commitment to digital wellness.

7. Foster a Supportive Environment

- Encourage Accountability: Share your goals with friends or family members who can help hold you accountable. Consider forming a support group focused on digital wellness.

- Create a Culture of Wellness: In workplace settings, promote a culture that values digital wellness. This includes setting clear expectations regarding after-hours communication and encouraging regular breaks.

8. Reflect on Long-Term Impact

- Evaluate Overall Well-Being: Regularly assess how your digital habits affect your mental, emotional, and physical health. Consider conducting surveys or self-assessments to gauge your progress.

- Adapt to Life Changes: Recognize that your digital wellness needs may change over time due to life circumstances, work demands, or personal growth. Be prepared to adjust your strategies accordingly.

By actively monitoring your progress and being willing to adjust your strategies, you can create a sustainable digital wellness plan that enhances your overall quality of life and helps you maintain a healthy relationship with technology.

Conclusion: Thriving in the Digital Age:

As we navigate the complexities of the digital age, thriving requires a proactive approach to managing our relationship with technology. The integration of digital tools into our personal and professional lives offers immense opportunities for growth, connection, and innovation. However, it also presents challenges that necessitate a mindful and strategic approach to digital wellness.

Embracing Digital Transformation

To thrive in this environment, individuals and organizations must embrace digital transformation. This involves not only adopting new technologies but also rethinking how we interact with them. Key strategies include:

- Enhancing User Experience: Prioritizing user-centric design in digital tools ensures that technology enhances rather than detracts from our daily lives. This means creating intuitive interfaces and seamless interactions that cater to user needs.

- Fostering Digital Literacy: Continuous education about digital tools and their impact is essential. By improving digital literacy, individuals can make informed choices about technology use, leading to healthier habits and reduced digital overload.

- Promoting a Balanced Approach: It's crucial to establish boundaries around technology use. Implementing strategies such as digital detoxes, tech-free zones, and mindful engagement can help mitigate the negative effects of excessive screen time.

Building Resilience and Adaptability

In a rapidly changing digital landscape, resilience and adaptability are vital. This can be achieved through:

- Setting Realistic Goals: Individuals should set achievable digital wellness goals that align with their lifestyles. Gradually implementing changes allows for sustainable habits that can evolve over time.

- Monitoring Progress: Regularly assessing digital habits and their impact on well-being helps identify areas for improvement. This ongoing reflection enables individuals to adjust their strategies and stay on track.

- Encouraging Community Support: Engaging with peers, family, and colleagues in discussions about digital wellness fosters a supportive environment. Sharing experiences and strategies can enhance collective resilience.

Prioritizing Well-Being

Ultimately, thriving in the digital age hinges on prioritizing well-being. This involves:

- Balancing Technology with Human Connection: While technology facilitates communication, it's essential to nurture face-to-face interactions and meaningful relationships. Striking a balance between digital and real-life connections enhances emotional well-being.

- Emphasizing Mental Health: Recognizing the impact of digital habits on mental health is crucial. Implementing practices such as mindfulness, self-care, and stress management can help individuals maintain a healthy mindset amidst digital distractions.

- Championing Ethical Technology Use: As we embrace digital tools, it's important to advocate for ethical practices in technology development and usage. This includes promoting privacy, security, and inclusivity to ensure that technology serves the greater good.

Looking Ahead

As we move forward, the ability to thrive in the digital age will depend on our commitment to cultivating a healthy relationship with technology. By embracing digital transformation, building resilience, and prioritizing well-being, we can harness the power of technology to enhance our lives while mitigating its challenges. The journey towards digital wellness is ongoing, and with intentionality and support, we can navigate this landscape successfully, ensuring that technology enriches our lives rather than detracts from them.

Appendices:

The appendices provide additional resources, tools, and references to support your journey toward digital wellness. These materials are designed to enhance your understanding and implementation of the concepts discussed throughout the book.

Appendix A: Digital Wellness Resources

Books
- "Digital Minimalism" by Cal Newport: A guide to finding focus and meaning in a distracted world.
- "How to Break Up with Your Phone" by Catherine Price: A practical guide to reducing phone dependency and improving your relationship with technology.
- "The Shallows: What the Internet Is Doing to Our Brains" by Nicholas Carr: An exploration of how the internet affects cognitive abilities and attention spans.

Websites and Blogs
- Digital Wellness Collective: A community and resource hub focused on promoting digital wellness.
- Mindful Techie: A blog that offers insights and practices for mindful technology use.
- Common Sense Media: A resource for parents and educators on media and technology use for children and teens.

Apps
- Forest: An app that encourages focus by planting virtual trees as you stay off your phone.
- Moment: Tracks your screen time and helps you set goals for reducing it.
- Headspace: A mindfulness and meditation app that promotes mental well-being.

Appendix B: Sample Digital Wellness Plan Template:

Personal Digital Wellness Plan

Name:
Date:

Current Digital Habits
- Average daily screen time:
- Primary devices used:
- Common activities (e.g., social media, gaming, work):

Goals
1. Specific Goal:
   - Description:
   - Measurable Outcome:
   - Deadline:

2. Specific Goal:
   - Description:
   - Measurable Outcome:
   - Deadline:

Action Steps
1. Action Step for Goal 1:
   - Task:
   - Timeline:

2. Action Step for Goal 2:
   - Task:
   - Timeline:

Monitoring and Reflection
- Check-in Dates:
1.
2.
3.

- Reflections on Progress:
- Adjustments Needed:

Appendix C: Digital Wellness Assessment Questionnaire

Digital Wellness Self-Assessment

1. Screen Time:
   - On average, how many hours per day do you spend on screens (including phone, computer, and TV)?
   - Do you feel this amount of screen time is too much, too little, or just right?

2. Social Media Use:
   - How many social media platforms do you actively use?
   - Do you find social media enhances or detracts from your well-being?

3. Work-Life Balance:
   - Do you often check work emails or messages outside of work hours?
   - How does this affect your personal time and relationships?

4. Mental Health:
   - How often do you feel overwhelmed or anxious due to technology use?
   - Do you have strategies in place to manage digital stress?

5. Physical Health:
   - Do you experience any physical discomfort (e.g., eye strain, headaches) related to screen use?
   - How often do you take breaks from screens?

Appendix D: Additional Reading and References

Articles and Research Papers

- "The Impact of Digital Technology on Mental Health": A review of current research on technology's effects on mental health.
- "Screen Time and Children: What the Research Says": An overview of studies on screen time recommendations for children and adolescents.

Organizations
- American Psychological Association (APA): Resources on the psychological effects of technology.
- World Health Organization (WHO): Guidelines on digital health and well-being.

Appendix E: Glossary of Terms

- Digital Wellness: A state of physical, mental, and social well-being in relation to technology use.
- Screen Time: The amount of time spent using devices with screens, such as computers, smartphones, and televisions.
- Mindfulness: The practice of being present and fully engaged in the moment, often used to reduce stress and improve focus.
- Digital Detox: A period of time during which a person refrains from using digital devices to focus on real-life interactions and activities.

These appendices serve as a comprehensive resource for further exploration of digital wellness concepts and practices. By utilizing these tools and insights, you can continue your journey toward a healthier, more balanced relationship with technology.

Glossary of Digital Terms:

This glossary provides definitions and explanations of key terms related to digital wellness, technology use, and online behavior. Understanding these terms is essential for navigating the digital landscape effectively.

1. Digital Wellness
A state of personal well-being achieved through the healthy use of digital technology. It involves crafting a balanced relationship with technology that enhances health and happiness rather than detracting from it.

2. Screen Time
The amount of time spent using devices with screens, such as smartphones, tablets, computers, and televisions. Monitoring screen time is essential for assessing digital habits and their impact on well-being.

3. Digital Detox
A period during which an individual refrains from using digital devices to reduce stress and focus on real-life interactions and activities. This practice aims to reset one's relationship with technology.

4. Digital Literacy
The ability to effectively use, understand, and critically evaluate digital technologies. It encompasses skills such as navigating the internet, using software applications, and understanding online safety.

5. Digital Citizenship
Engaging in responsible and respectful online behavior. This includes understanding rights and responsibilities as a digital user, respecting others' privacy, and fostering positive online interactions.

6. Digital Safety
Measures taken to protect oneself from online risks, such as cyberbullying, privacy violations, and misinformation. This involves recognizing potential threats and managing them effectively.

7. Digital Health
The influence of digital technology on physical, mental, and emotional health. It includes managing the adverse effects of excessive screen time and using technology to enhance overall well-being.

8. Mindfulness
The practice of being present and fully engaged in the moment, which can help reduce stress and improve focus. Mindfulness techniques can be applied to technology use to promote healthier habits.

9. Digital Overload
A state of feeling overwhelmed by the amount of information and notifications received through digital devices. This can lead to stress, distraction, and decreased productivity.

10. Digital Flourishing
A concept that represents the optimal state where productivity, health, and happiness align through effective technology use. It emphasizes the positive impact of technology on overall well-being.

11. Cyberbullying
The use of digital platforms to harass, threaten, or intimidate individuals. It can have severe psychological effects on victims and is a significant concern in digital environments.

12. Telemedicine
The use of digital technology to provide healthcare services remotely. This includes virtual consultations, remote monitoring, and online health resources, improving access to care.

13. Online Therapy
Mental health support provided through digital platforms, including video calls, chat, or apps. It offers accessible options for individuals seeking psychological help.

14. Social Media Literacy
The ability to navigate, understand, and critically evaluate content on social media platforms. This includes recognizing misinformation and understanding the impact of social media on mental health.

15. Digital Participation
Engagement in online activities, including social networking, online learning, and digital communication. It encompasses both the benefits and potential risks associated with being active in digital spaces.

16. Digital Wellbeing Industry
The growing market for software, hardware, and services aimed at promoting mental health and well-being through digital tools. This includes apps for mindfulness, productivity, and mental health support.

17. Behavioral Addiction
A condition where an individual becomes compulsively engaged in a behavior, such as excessive gaming or internet use, leading to negative consequences in daily life.

18. Privacy Settings
Options provided by digital platforms that allow users to control who can see their information and how it is shared. Understanding and managing privacy settings is crucial for protecting personal data.

19. Digital Footprint
The trail of data left by an individual's online activities, including social media posts, website visits, and online purchases. It is important to be aware of one's digital footprint for privacy and security.

20. Content Moderation
The process of monitoring and managing user-generated content on digital platforms to ensure compliance with community standards and to prevent harmful behavior.

This glossary serves as a foundational resource for understanding the terminology associated with digital wellness and technology use. Familiarity with these terms can empower individuals to navigate the digital landscape more effectively and cultivate healthier digital habits.

Recommended apps and tools for digital wellness:

Here are some recommended apps and tools for digital wellness, based on the search results:

Recommended Apps for Digital Wellness

1. ActionDash
   - Price: Free
   - Features: Provides insights into screen time and app usage, encourages users to cut down on screen time, and allows users to lock themselves out of apps to promote healthier habits.

2. Digital Detox
   - Price: Free
   - Features: Offers various challenge modes to help reduce screen time. It utilizes device administrator permissions to limit phone usage and promotes accountability through challenges.

3. Digitox
   - Price: Free / $5.00
   - Features: Tracks app usage and time spent on devices, allows users to set timers, and provides warnings when limits are reached. It also calculates productive time spent on work-related tasks.

4. Forest
   - Price: Free with in-app purchases
   - Features: A focus timer that gamifies staying off your phone. Users set a timer, and if they adhere to it, a virtual tree grows. Checking the phone during the timer kills the tree, encouraging focus.

5. Google Family Link
   - Price: Free
   - Features: Allows parents to manage their children's device usage, set screen time limits, and monitor app activity to promote healthy digital habits.

6. Calm
   - Price: Free with subscription options
   - Features: Offers meditation, sleep stories, and mindfulness exercises to promote relaxation and mental well-being.

7. MyFitnessPal
   - Price: Free with premium features
   - Features: A comprehensive app for tracking nutrition, fitness goals, and overall health. It encourages users to maintain a balanced lifestyle.

8. Headspace
   - Price: Free with subscription options
   - Features: Provides guided meditation and mindfulness practices to help reduce stress and improve mental clarity.

9. Moment
   - Price: Free / Premium version available
   - Features: Tracks how much time you spend on your phone and helps set daily limits to reduce screen time.

10. Flipd
   - Price: Free / Premium version available
   - Features: Encourages users to stay off their phones by locking them out of distracting apps for set periods. It also includes a community feature for accountability.

Tools for Digital Wellbeing

- Android Digital Wellbeing Tools: Built into modern Android devices, these tools provide insights into app usage, allow users to set timers, and enable features like Focus Mode and Bedtime Mode to minimize distractions.

- Focus Mode: A feature that pauses selected apps to help users concentrate on tasks without interruptions.

- Do Not Disturb: A setting that silences notifications and alerts, allowing users to focus or relax without distractions.

- Snooze Notifications: Temporarily hides notifications from specific apps to minimize distractions during focused work or relaxation periods.

These apps and tools can help individuals manage their digital habits, promote mindfulness, and enhance overall digital wellness. By incorporating these resources into daily routines, users can cultivate healthier relationships with technology and improve their well-being.

Self-assessment quizzes:

Here are some self-assessment quizzes that can help you evaluate your digital wellness and understand your relationship with technology:

1. Digital Wellness @ Work™ Quiz
   - Offered by Digitally Well, this quiz assesses your digital wellness in the workplace. It helps you understand how technology impacts your personal well-being and workplace performance.
   - After completing the quiz, you will receive a personalized report via email that provides insights into your digital habits and suggestions for improvement.
   - Take the quiz here (https://digitallywell.ca/self-assessment-hub/).

2. Virtual Emotional Intelligence™ Quiz
   - Also provided by Digitally Well, this quiz evaluates your emotional intelligence skills in a virtual context. It focuses on five dimensions: self-awareness, self-regulation, motivation, empathy, and social skills.
   - A detailed report will be sent to you after completion, highlighting areas for growth and development in your virtual interactions.
   - Explore the quiz here (https://digitallywell.ca/self-assessment-hub/).

3. Digital Wellbeing Self-Assessment
   - Available on Voxel Hub, this online assessment features questions about your digital habits across six core aspects of digital well-being.
   - You will rate your experiences on a scale from thriving to struggling, and receive educational tips and insights after each section.
   - This assessment allows you to track your progress over time and reflect on your digital habits.
   - Access the self-assessment here (https://voxelhub.org/digital-wellbeing-self-assessment/).

4. Digital Wellbeing Assessment by Charity for Civil Servants
   - This survey helps you evaluate your digital habits and their impact on your well-being. It covers six key areas: Wellbeing, Boundary, Communication, Focus, Connection, and Purpose.

- The assessment aims to provide a snapshot of how technology is affecting your life, enabling you to make informed adjustments.
   - Take the survey here (https://www.cfcs.org.uk/help-advice/health-and-wellbeing/wellbeing-at-work/digital-wellbeing/).

These quizzes and assessments are valuable tools for gaining insights into your digital habits and identifying areas for improvement. By reflecting on your relationship with technology, you can develop a more balanced and healthy approach to digital wellness.

Here are some worksheets and templates for personal planning that can help you organize your goals and enhance your digital wellness journey:

1. Personal Planning Templates by Microsoft
- Description: Microsoft offers a variety of customizable personal planning templates, including personal development plans, daily schedules, and five-year plans.
- Features: You can easily edit these templates in Microsoft Word or Excel, allowing you to tailor them to your specific needs. Once customized, you can download, print, or share them.
- Access: Explore Microsoft Personal Planning Templates (https://create.microsoft.com/en-us/templates/personal-planning).

2. ELSA Individual Planning Template Pack
- Description: This pack includes fillable forms designed for one-on-one sessions, ideal for educators or individuals looking to plan effectively.
- Included Templates:
  - Individual session planning sheet
  - Six-week overview for session planning
  - Individual assessment record
- Features: The templates are fillable and can be easily edited on a computer, making organization straightforward.
- Purchase: Available for £2.50 at ELSA Support (https://www.elsa-support.co.uk/resources/elsa-individual-planning-template-pack-item-488/).

3. Budget Planning Templates by StepChange
- Description: StepChange provides free budgeting templates to help you manage your finances effectively.
- Features: These templates allow you to list monthly income and expenses, helping you identify areas for savings and better financial planning.
- Access: Get Free Budget Templates (https://www.stepchange.org/debt-info/how-to-make-a-budget.aspx).

4. Digital Habits Checkup from Harvard Project Zero
- Description: This self-assessment tool helps individuals evaluate their digital habits and make positive changes to support well-being.
- Features: The checkup encourages reflection on personal digital usage and can be used in various educational settings.
- Access: Download the Digital Habits Checkup
(https://pz.harvard.edu/sites/default/files/Digital%20Habits%20Checkup_0.pdf).

5. Self-Assessment Hub by Digitally Well
- Description: This hub offers various assessments to evaluate your digital wellness at work and your emotional intelligence in virtual settings.
- Features: After completing the quizzes, you receive personalized reports that provide insights and suggestions for improvement.
- Access: Visit the Self-Assessment Hub (https://digitallywell.ca/self-assessment-hub/).

These worksheets and templates can assist you in setting clear goals, tracking your progress, and enhancing your overall digital wellness. By utilizing these resources, you can create a structured approach to managing your digital habits and achieving your personal objectives.

Recommended readings and resources for further exploration of digital wellness:

Books

1. Digital Minimalism: Choosing a Focused Life in a Noisy World by Cal Newport
 - This book explores how to minimize distractions and focus on what truly matters in a digitally saturated world. Newport offers practical strategies for reducing technology's impact on daily life.

2. Deep Work: Rules for Focused Success in a Distracted World by Cal Newport
 - A modern classic that emphasizes the importance of focused work and offers strategies for cultivating deep concentration in an age of constant distractions.

3. Indistractable: How to Control Your Attention and Choose Your Life by Nir Eyal
 - Eyal discusses how to manage distractions and take control of your attention, providing actionable insights for using technology in a way that serves your goals.

4. Alone Together: Why We Expect More from Technology and Less from Each Other by Sherry Turkle
 - This book examines the paradox of feeling more connected through technology while experiencing increased loneliness. Turkle explores the implications of our digital interactions on relationships.

5. The Shallows: What the Internet Is Doing to Our Brains by Nicholas Carr
 - Carr investigates how the internet affects cognitive functions, arguing that constant connectivity can diminish our ability to think deeply and critically.

6. The Joy of Missing Out: Finding Balance in a Wired World by Christina Crook
 - Crook offers insights into how to embrace a more intentional and fulfilling life by disconnecting from the digital world and focusing on real-life experiences.

Articles and Research Papers

1. "Digital Wellbeing: The Need of the Hour in Today's Digitalized and Technology Driven World"

- This article discusses the challenges of adhering to digital wellness practices and the importance of personalizing digital well-being strategies to meet individual needs. Read the article here (https://www.ncbi.nlm.nih.gov/pmc/articles/PMC9446377/).

2. "A Guide to Digital Wellness in the Workplace: Why it Matters"
   - This guide offers strategies for promoting digital wellness in workplace settings, including workshops, assessments, and creating a supportive environment. Explore the guide here (https://www.masteryoursea.com/post/digital-wellness).

Online Resources

1. Goodreads Digital Wellness Shelf
   - A collection of popular books on digital wellness, providing user ratings and reviews to help you choose the right reading material. Visit Goodreads (https://www.goodreads.com/shelf/show/digital-wellness).

2. Digital Wellness Collective
   - A community dedicated to promoting digital wellness through resources, events, and educational materials. Join the community (https://digitalwellnesscollective.org/).

3. Mindful Techie
   - A blog that offers insights and practices for mindful technology use, focusing on how to create a balanced digital lifestyle. Visit Mindful Techie (https://mindfultechie.com/).

These resources provide valuable insights and practical strategies for understanding and improving digital wellness, helping you navigate the complexities of technology in today's world.